Storytelling with Music, Puppets, and Arts

William Painter with large friend

Storytelling

with Music, Puppets, and Arts
for Libraries and Classrooms

by

William M. Painter

Library Professional Publications
1994

Library of Congress Cataloging-in-Publication Data

Painter, William M., 1941–
Storytelling with music, puppets, and arts
for libraries and classrooms / by William M. Painter.
p.   cm.
Includes bibliographical references.
ISBN 0-208-02372-0 (alk. paper)
1. Storytelling.   2. Children's libraries—Activity programs.
3. Oral reading.   I. Title.
Z718.3.P36   1994
027.62′51—dc20   94-20096
                                                                              CIP

*The paper in this publication meets the minimum requirements of
American National Standard
for Information Science—Permanence of Paper
for Printed Library Materials, ANSI Z39.48—1984.* ⊗

12/4/95   sben AGD1035

Printed in the United States of America

Contents

Introduction

An editorial in the *Miami Herald* once described modern research which found that "the single most important factor influencing success in school was being read to." Headlined "Reading to Children Is More Than Child's Play," this appeared back in the December 3, 1985 issue of the paper—most copies of which have certainly been dumped unceremoniously in the trash by now.

One of our library patrons, however, clipped the article from her copy of the morning paper. Being a professional picture framer, she matted it, framed it beautifully under glass, and presented it to our public library here in North Miami. We promptly hung it in the children's room.

That editorial on our library wall becomes more relevant with each passing year. Since it was written, people have become increasingly anxious about finding ways to deal with the problems of high illiteracy and frightening school dropout rates.

Certainly one thing, and the very best and most effective thing to do to counteract these trends, is to read to children *early on*, in a *regular way*, and help them to *connect* what is being read to them to the world around them through reading exercises.

My first two books, *Musical Story Hours* and *Story Hours with Puppets and Other Props* do this by first, using classical and popular music as background for read-alouds in story hour; and second, by adding puppets and stuffed animals to the basic story presentation, whether read or told. These devices help to increase the attention spans of preschoolers and early elementary school students so I can read more and longer.

In this book, I capitalize on that increased attention by adding more activities to my programs—simple things such as conversations and games for the preschoolers; and more advanced activities for the early grades, such as creative writing based on the music, or interpreting music through drawings or connecting famous art works to the themes of music or stories. Certainly these are things that could be done in places other than the public library: in the classroom, the daycare group, the play group, a Headstart program—nearly anywhere that young children are cared for in groups by loving adults.

But lack of interest in reading and poor reading skills are not the only things that have surfaced since that editorial in the mid–80s. With changing economic times, creative writing and the fine arts—music, art, and drama—have usually been the first programs to be cut from money-starved public school budgets. In many cities, towns, and even states, children are going without even basic exposure—let alone instruction—in the very things that can enrich a child's life beyond the usual success-oriented or competitive academic courses. Some children will not have the chance to hear a piece of classical music or to draw a picture of their *own* starry night; many will not be encouraged to let their minds wander into poetry, or to close their eyes and imagine a herd of horses galloping across a plain. But if teachers, librarians, storytellers, and other youth leaders learn to incorporate such experiences into everyday sessions with books, these things will not be denied them.

Musical backgrounds have been used in films all along, mainly to help create mood and heighten interest. Think of the romantic aura that the "Unchained Melody" spun around Demi Moore and Patrick Swayze in *Ghost*. Think of the fifties' atmosphere created in *American Graffiti* by the continuous Wolfman Jack radio show in the background, with all the rock-and-roll hits from the era. Mozart's tender and wistful slow movement of the "Piano Concerto no. 21" was so dramatically paired with the ill-fated lovers in the movie *Elvira Madigan* that it is advertised on cassette covers as the *Elvira Madigan* concerto. Can you imagine how much of the mood and atmosphere would be lost if the lush, majestic background music were taken out of *Gone with the*

Wind or *Doctor Zhivago*, or if the peppy Rossini *Barber of Seville* overture were absent from the bicycle-racing sequences of *Breaking Away?*

There's no valid reason that we story readers and tellers can't use musical backgrounds in our story times to help create our own moods and atmospheres, just as the moviemakers do. Well-known librarian and storyteller Spencer Shaw was doing this back in the 1950s in Brooklyn, New York, so it is certainly not a new idea. You just have to keep the music low enough to remain as background to the storyteller's voice.

Here is an example of what I mean. It's interesting to ask children if they have ever heard Beethoven's "Moonlight Sonata" ("Piano Sonata no. 14") or if they know it by name. Chances are good that few have. You could us it with several types of stories. The slow, haunting opening movement can be used as background for any number of dark and spooky children's stories, where mystery and suspense are created. *The Spooky Eerie Night Noise* by Mona Rabun Reeves, for instance, described in delicious detail the imaginary monsters two children conjure up when they hear strange sounds coming from their dark back yard. (Don't worry. The noises were from the harmless skunks.)

It can also weave a quiet, romantic spell as Edward Lear's *Owl and the Pussycat* dance in the light of their moon. Or, it could create the anticipation and terror of Ichabod Crane from Washington Irving's "Legend of Sleepy Hollow" as he watches for the Headless Horseman to appear. In using the "Moonlight Sonata" in these ways, you are not only creating your mood or atmosphere and enhancing your storytelling, you may also be serving as a music appreciation teacher providing a first experience of this lovely piece of music.

You may not be a music scholar, but a little basic research on Beethoven would enable you also to build on "Moonlight Sonata" in other ways. For example, you could pass along a lesson in dealing with handicaps. The composer began to go deaf in 1801 and eventually lost all hearing. "I will seize fate by the throat. It shall certainly never overcome me," Beethoven said defiantly. Many of his greatest works were composed while he was nearly or completely deaf. (A good source for such basic information is David Ewen's *Great Composers, 1300 to 1900.*)

I have tried to include cassette tapes, records, and compact disc versions of music in this book. Generally, however, you can find the music in whatever form you are best able to use. If your budget is limited (like mine), you may be forced to stick with tapes and records.

You can also be an art teacher of sorts by showing the children some famous "night" paintings, such as Van Gogh's *Starry Night* and Whistler's *Battersea Bridge; Nocturne in Blue.* Then have the children draw their *own* pictures of a moonlit night. You can exhibit these on the walls of your library or classroom, perhaps with pictures by "other famous artists." It will add to the children's pride in their own efforts and to their understanding of the efforts of others.

Many public libraries have circulating framed art print collections which you can draw from. Art books are another prime resource. Showing the Van Gogh would give you a chance to touch on expressionism in art. Point out that the swirling rendering of Van Gogh's sky is not a photographic depiction. It is an *expression* of how the artist felt about the scene. You can introduce the concept that art does not have to be realistic, and that imaginative interpretations are legitimate forms of expression.

If anyone thinks the idea of using adult art works with children's storytelling is far out, let me point out that it's been done long before I started. Back in 1985, for example, the Metropolitan Museum of Art put out a book called *Talking to the Sun: An Illustrated Anthology of Poems for Young People.* The poems are accompanied by pictures of paintings, sculptures, and other treasures from the Metropolitan. For example, the song "Greensleeves" is paired with two pieces of German porcelain depicting two couples. Tennyson's poem, "The Letter," describing a love letter from a shy suitor, is paired with Fragonard's painting, *The Love Letter.* An "Oath of Friendship" penned in China is matched with a statue from the Fifth Dynasty of Egypt ca. 2360 B.C. Edna St. Vincent Millay's poem, "Afternoon on a Hill," is shown with Monet's painting *Apple Trees in Bloom.* I've used a Monet painting in this book as well.

A second, more recent book using great art works with very young preschoolers is *I Spy—An Alphabet in Art,* devised and selected by Lucy Micklethwait. She points out that most art books are found "out of reach, but this one is for the picture book shelf." Micklethwait began playing this artistic version of "I Spy" with her own young children, taking a look at great paintings and finding objects which begin with certain letters of the alphabet. What can be found in Jan Van Eyck's painting, *The Arnolfini Marriage,* for example, that begins with a "D"? There is, you will see, a cute little dog standing between the couple holding hands in this famous painting.

Ms. Micklethwait is not afraid to use both paintings from centuries ago and very modern ones with preschoolers. David Hockney's contemporary *A Bigger Splash* illustrates "W" for water; Magritte's *Son of Man* shows an apple ("A) suspended directly in front of the face of a businessman in a suit and tie. Moving back several centuries, Wybrand de Geest's *Portrait of a Child* gives us a "Z" (many of them) in the pattern of the young girl's dress. The time warp moves forward all the way to Picasso's ultra-modern *Woman with a Fish Hat* ("F" for fish). Henri Rousseau's *The Football Players* shows us a ball for our "B," and proves that football goes back quite a way before Joe Montana and Dan Marino.

The concept of using great art with very young children is certainly one which can be explored in many enriching, imaginative ways, as *I Spy* reminds us. I feel the same way about this as I do about using classical music with two and three-year-olds: it works, it is enriching, it is enjoyable, and it is not something to shy away from in favor of "children's" music or art.

What about creative writing? You can venture into this with middle or upper elementary children or students. They could write a short, spooky mystery story set in the moonlight. If you read up on short story writing, you can introduce the basics of characters, plot, problem and resolution, description, and theme. Of course, this would not work well with your preschoolers or early elementary pupils. You may have some third graders who could handle such activities.

You can pack children into a public library story hour program each week, or you can create and hold the interest of a class full of them in a school or daycare center by adding a few puppets and stuffed animals (or toys) in the background of your story presentation. Children, library workers, teacher aides, parents, or other volunteers can be used as puppeteers. Think of all the stuffed monsters you can find, for example, with Reeves's book, *The Spooky, Eerie Night Noise*. A formal puppet stage or an overturned table covered with a blanket can create instant magic. Don't wait to be formal.

Certainly you might well be sowing some seeds of influence with such activities. Theory and practice show that each enriches the other and contributes towards children's abilities to use and understand written and oral language, to express themselves through, and understand, art and music. Besides fostering these skills, you may also interest someone in taking up a pen or pastels or a paintbrush, puppets or a musical instrument, in earnest. But whatever might come of these enriched story hours, you will know that you are offering children a pathway--sometimes the *only* pathway—to a lifelong enjoyment of creative endeavor.

References

Books:

Koch, Kenneth and Kate Farrell, compilers. *Talking to the Sun: An Illustrated Anthology of Poems for Young People.* Metropolitan Museum of Art/Henry Holt, 1985.
Micklethwait, Lucy. *I Spy—An Alphabet in Art.* Greenwillow, 1991.

Compact Disc:

Beethoven, Ludwig van. "Piano Sonata no. 14" ("Moonlight Sonata"). *Beethoven—Greatest Hits.* R.C.A. 0-9026-60831-2. (Available in numerous compact disc, cassette tape, and recording versions.)

1

Harp Music and Storytelling

I certainly didn't originate the idea of liberally adding music to story hours, but I just may be the first to ever combine the light and bouncy *Adante Allegro* opening movement of Handel's "Concerto in B-flat for Harp, Strings and Two Flutes" with Gene Zion's light, happy, and bouncy story, *Harry the Dirty Dog*. All you need is a little imagination and you, too, can make such unlikely pairings.

Harp music is particularly good for using with storytelling because it tends to stay in the background and not overwhelm the teller. Let's launch right into a real exploration of harp music and children's stories using the cassette tape, *Favourite Harp Concertos*.

If you have ever been to Walt Disney World's Epcot Center in Florida, you may well have heard one of the harp selections on this cassette. In Epcot's recreated "France" (in the international section), there is a travel film on the country with a magnificent soundtrack from the works of French composers. The camera sweeps by from different heights and angles along the wall of white cliffs on the coast, offering breathtaking aerial views of the majestic formations. You, the viewer, are also swept along by the airy, swirling sounds of Boieldieu's "Concerto in C for Harp and Orchestra," the third movement, or "Rondeau" (*Allegro Agitato*).

Once I found out what the music was and purchased the tape, I began to look for stories about birds or flight or motion, to try in combination with the music. I decided on two fantastic picture books by Chris Van Allsburg, which were such dramatically perfect counterparts to the music I couldn't wait to try them out.

✳ ✳ ✳

The Polar Express is the 1985 Caldecott Award-winning book about a mysterious train that pulls up to a boy's front door to take him to the North Pole at Christmas time. The boy had been told that there was no Santa Claus; this train will let him see for himself.

The train goes faster and faster up and down hills and high mountains through gently falling flakes of snow. Most of the journey blends in perfectly with the harp music, which evokes this motion over hills and curves and dips and ascents, and gives the impression of speed. Harp strings being plucked rapidly suggest falling snowflakes, and the music has a haunting quality, both melodic and spellbinding. The story, too, shares this quality of fantasy made concrete and believable.

This is such a perfect musical match. You should experience it alone first so you can understand its effect before trying it with a group of preschoolers or primary grade children. Read the story aloud while you are alone with the music. You will see what possibilities exist.

In *The Polar Express*, Santa selects this boy as the child who will receive the first Christmas present of the year. He chooses a bell from the harness of one of the reindeer. On the train ride home, the other pajama-clad children ask to see it. The boy reaches into his pocket and discovers a hole. No bell. Heartbroken, he returns home, to find a small present under the Christmas tree. It is a reindeer harness bell—from "Mr. C." His parents can't hear its beautiful sound, and the boy's friends can only hear it for a few years.

The boy himself grows old, too, but he can still hear the lovely sound, as can all who truly do believe.

It is not really necessary here to use background puppets to act out this story. Van Allsburg's pictures are such an integral and essential part of the story, and convey the hushed mystery of this magical experience, puppets would only detract. The story reader, the book, and the music are a good and simple combination. One technical point to consider, though, is the timing of music and story. The music is six minutes long, so you might want to practice coordinating your reading so as not to let the magic of the experience dribble away.

✳ ✳ ✳

Another piece of harp music on the tape of *Favourite Harp Concertos* which gives the impression of motion and flight is the finale movement of Petrini's "Concerto no. 4 in E-flat for Harp and Orchestra" (*Allegro*). It has a similar rapid pace with plenty of dips and dives in the melodies. Leo Lionni's *Tico and the Golden Wings* is a story which goes well with this or with the Boieldieu piece.

Lionni's bird character, Tico, cannot fly at all at the story's beginning, so you may want to hold the music until he gets his wings. Poor Tico has no wings at all, and his friends have to fly into the high tree branches to bring him berries. He dreams of having golden wings, and soon a pale blue "Wishingbird" appears, granting his wish.

With the ability to fly comes both joy and sadness. He does have golden wings, at least for a short while, but the other birds are angry because they feel he has been made "better" than they are.

Tico meets a poor basketmaker who cannot afford medicine for his sick child. The bird offers one of his golden wings, and thereby saves the child. A black wing suddenly grows where the golden one had been.

The acts of charity and goodness continue: the bird flies on to an old woman, a fisherman, and a bride—giving golden feathers to meet their various needs at each stop. My favorite is the one where the bird sells a golden feather for three new puppets for a poor puppeteer. Since I generally have puppets behind me on stage while I tell the stories out front, I can act the part of the poor puppeteer (very authentically) as I talk. Behind me the volunteers and staff members who serve as puppeteers have to do some quick changes on the bird puppet, regarding those wing colors, throughout this story. A black feather replaces a golden one, as each gold feather is given away. (Poster board versions of feathers can be used, or bags full of colored feathers can be purchased at novelty stores.)

* * *

Let's return to Chris Van Allsburg for a look at another fantasy book—*The Wreck of the Zephyr*.

Let's also begin to expand on our harp selections and use Mozart's famous "Flute and Harp Concerto." If you are familiar with James Galway, the popular flutist who often appears on television, you'll know that much of what he plays is especially exuberant and lively. That's why I chose his recording of the Mozart piece.

In *The Wreck of the Zephyr*, we see an older gentleman explaining the legend behind a beached sailboat to an inquisitive boy. It seems there once was another boy who begged some sailors to teach him how to sail the boat just as they did—above the clouds!

The boy persuades the sailors, but his attempt to fly fails. He returns by night, however, to try it again on his own. This time he gets the ship up and away, over the waves and over the clouds—at least until he crashes—and thus creates his legend.

Once again, *allegro*-speed harp music—in this case, the third movement "Rondo" (*Allegro*)—can very well give an illusion of motion and speed. Fast flute music does the same. The combination works well with the story, which has several things in motion at once—the ship, the water, the air, and the clouds. As with *The Polar Express*, adding puppets would be difficult and not necessary.

* * *

Let's take off in another direction now: Let's look at how a story such as *The Wreck of the Zephyr* can be tied in with other arts. Boys and boats. Chris Van Allsburg's theme had attracted many an earlier artist's attention as well.

At an exhibition of Winslow Homer's wood engravings and watercolors at Miami's new art institute, I noticed that in 1873 the American artist from Prout's Neck, Maine, did a wood engraving called *Ship Building in Gloucester Harbor*. It depicts a group of boys sitting on the ground carving wooden ship models in front of some workingmen actually building a large boat. Homer, with his studio right on the Maine seacoast, was drawn to such themes. He took the scene and painted a watercolor version, which he called *Boat Builders*. A reproduction of this painting appears in D. Scott Anderson's *Winslow Homer in Gloucester* as well as in many other books about the artist. This could be shown to children in a library or classroom as an example of a "boys and boats" theme explored by a great American artist. Four-year-olds are not too young to gaze at such paintings.

If you could get ahold of a *Harper's Weekly* illustration by Homer, you could also point out that he, like Chris Van Allsburg a century later, was also an illustrator. This will give you the chance to discuss illustrating a text versus painting a picture in its own right. This would be appropriate for older story hour kids—probably third grade and up. The flying ship of Chris Van Allsburg can also lead from the actual and model shipbuilders of Winslow Homer to the flights of fancy of Marc Chagall.

Chagall and Van Allsburg have a couple of things in common: both make things fly and both have done book illustrations. With Chagall, everything can fly—people, goats, buildings, flowers. The objects of the real world become enchanted in the colorful, imaginative, and exuberant cheerfulness of Chagall's visions of the world. Using some Chagall reproductions can be a fun way of introducing to children the concept that art does not have to be a realistic depiction, but is often a reflection of the artist's own special vision of the world.

An interesting theme, which you could also relate to *The Polar Express*, involves another artist who has something in common with Chris Van Allsburg. If you get ahold of some books with Norman Rockwell's *Saturday Evening Post* Santa Claus covers, you will see in the thoroughly convincing and realistic portraits that there are similarly convincing and life-like portrayals of Old Saint Nick!

You have an interesting writing topic from this for children who are old enough (fourth graders and older): "What is the favorite holiday or birthday present you ever received?" If the children are too young to write, this is fun to talk about instead. Even if the children in your group do not believe in Santa, they certainly will have something to say.

✳ ✳ ✳

The harp is just one of dozens of instruments, and concertos are just one musical form, that can combine with books to open up the arts for children. The possibilities are limitless and exciting, and are bound only by your imagination, your understanding of your audience, and your willingness to dig a little into the resources of your own library. Your own tastes and experimentations may lead you down other avenues. Good. You will begin then to form your own programs that will be right for the age and developmental levels of your group, and the needs of the community you serve. My suggestions here are just for "starters," and to hook you on these enriched and enriching programs.

A Sample Arts-Related Program
Theme: Flying: Boats, Trains, and Birds
Ages 4–8

1. *Participation song*
   "Row, Row, Row Your Boat"
   Ask, "But have you ever heard of a boat that could fly?"
2. *Musical story*
   Story: *The Wreck of the Zephyr* (Chris Van Allsburg)
   Music: "Flute and Harp Concerto," third movement (Mozart)
   Musical mood: Suggestive of motion—the flying boat, the water, the wind, the clouds.
   Art works: *The Boat Builders* (Homer); Chagall paintings with flying people and objects.
   Art project: Draw your family at home with someone or something flying.
3. *Participation song*
   "She'll Be Comin' Round the Mountain"
   Ask, "But have you ever seen a train fly?"
4. *Musical story*
   Story: *The Polar Express* (Chris Van Allsburg)
   Music: "Concerto in C for Harp and Orchestra," third movement (Boieldieu)
   Musical mood: Suggestive of flight, motion, speed, and snow.
   Art works: Norman Rockwell's Santas, on *Saturday Evening Post* covers.
   Essay or talk topic: "My favorite holiday or birthday present."
5. *Musical story*
   Say, "I know you've seen birds fly. Let's try a story about a bird."
   Story: *Tico and the Golden Wings* (Leo Lionni)
   Music: "Concerto no. 4 for Harp and Orchestra," second movement (Petrini)
   Musical mood: Suggestive of flight, thoughtful.

Puppets: Bird (plus poster-board gold and black feathers, or real ones), a second bird, three men, one old woman, one bride.

References

Books:

Lionni, Leo. *Tico and the Golden Wings*. Pantheon, 1964.
Van Allsburg, Chris. *The Polar Express*. Houghton Mifflin, 1985.
————. *The Wreck of the Zephyr*. Houghton Mifflin, 1983.
Zion, Gene. *Harry the Dirty Dog*. Harper & Row, 1956.

Cassettes:

Boieldieu, François. "Concerto in C for Harp and Orchestra." *Favourite Harp Concertos*. Philips 422 288–4.
Handel, George Frederic. "Concerto in B-flat for Harp, Strings and Two Flutes." *Favourite Harp Concertos*. Philips 422 288–4.
Mozart, Wolfgang Amadeus. *Mozart: Flute and Harp Concerto*. James Galway, flute. Fritz Heimis, harp. E.M.I./Angel 4AM–34723.
Petrini, Franz. "Concerto No. 4 in E-flat for Harp and Orchestra." *Favourite Harp Concertos*. Philips 422 288–4.

2

Puppetry and Hans Christian Andersen

We've started talking about adding various art forms to the act of storytelling, but now let's focus on one—the art of puppetry. I love to combine puppets with my storytelling and, every year, the puppets seem to offer me new ways to use them!

First of all, I generally tell the story myself in front of a stage. Stages can be purchased or built or, in many cases, improvised. A blanket or large piece of cloth thrown over an overturned table or a couple of chairs can serve as a stage. I've seen a puppet stage cut out of a new refrigerator cardboard packing box! I saw a teacher use a standing wooden bookcase as a puppet stage. Imagination and improvisation can take the place of a capital budget in this work!

I like to tell the story myself and let my volunteers mime parts of the story with the puppets, stuffed animals, dolls, wooden and plastic toys, and drawings on rods. Teachers can easily get volunteer students right out of their seats to work the puppets. Volunteers can also control the music. A simple cassette tape recorder (with batteries or electrical cord), or a compact disc player, can be used backstage if you don't have a stereo or room for large equipment.

✳ ✳ ✳

Let's take a look at what can be done with a Hans Christian Andersen story such as "The Swineherd." For many of the classic folktales, a basic collection of royalty puppets or dolls can be

15

practically all you need. A king, a queen, a prince, and a princess can give you a basic cast for hundreds of stories! The Nancy Renfro Studio, for example, sells a basic collection of royalty puppets and another collection of people puppets, both of which our library uses frequently.

In "The Swineherd," Andersen tells the story of a very vain princess and the only moderately-well-off prince who is courting her. The prince sends her a nightingale, which she rejects because it's real and not mechanical. He sends her a beautiful rose which she also rejects because it's real and not artificial. Rebuffed, the resourceful prince gets himself employed as a keeper of the pigs at her castle—that is, as a swineherd.

He makes a couple of odd little inventions in his spare time. The first is a pot which somehow lets you know what every woman in town is cooking for supper. The second is a rattle that plays waltzes and tunes. Although the vain princess had rejected the beautiful bird and flower, she simply must have these trifles.

The princess sends her ladies-in-waiting to ask the price of the pot. "Ten kisses," the swineherd-prince insists. Shocked, the princess offers ten from the ladies-in-waiting. The prince refuses: only the princess will do. She finally agrees.

After the prince collects his kisses and the princess collects her pot, she then learns about the musical rattle, and sends the ladies to ascertain the price. (I like to put on a Strauss waltz— such as "The Blue Danube"—when I introduce the rattle in the story. The melodic and well-known music fits well since the rattle's music is supposed to be irresistible.)

One hundred kisses—from the princess—is the non-negotiable cost. Eventually she agrees, but the king sees the two in action somewhere around kiss eighty and throws them both out of the castle. When the princess laments that she hadn't accepted the prince who gave her the rose and the bird previously, the swineherd reveals his identity. The joyful princess is all set to live happily ever after with him, but her joy is short: The prince rejects her because of her fickleness!

Since we already have the royal family puppets, we can bring in some creative props. Our library volunteer with nine children must have gone through quite a few cooking pots in her time, and she was more than willing to donate an old beat-up one for the swineherd's magical pot. A local 5– and 10–cent store in downtown Miami sells plastic flowers for a dollar a bunch, and the roses were plentiful. Someone had sent my parents a Christmas bouquet and there were a couple of styrofoam birds in there. One became the nightingale. Several staff members had babies a few years ago, so a donated baby rattle wasn't too hard to wrangle. I happen to have six pig puppets for the swine, but you could just as easily draw a few on poster board, color them in and cut them out. These can be taped to any kind of rods to hold up over the stage.

Teachers have told me that they like the idea of using music and puppets in their classrooms with storytelling, but they say that storage space is a concern. It is for me, too, but children respond so well to the puppets and music that lack of availability or storage space for a formal stage and stereo should not stop teachers, librarians, or daycare providers from trying to incorporate them. Librarians solve the storage problem by compacting puppets and stuffed animals in boxes. Another good storage idea is to hang a crocheted fishnet, made by volunteers or purchased at the 5 and 10, in a corner and fill it with your puppets and stuffed animals. Teachers can cooperate with other teachers in sharing closets and bookcases in more than one classroom. Another solution is to buy standing racks which hold many puppets from such companies as R. Dakin.

✳ ✳ ✳

Now, let's look at another Hans Christian Andersen story, "The Real Princess," and think about adding puppets and music to the telling.

"The Real Princess," of course, is also known as "The Princess and the Pea," and your first decision is whether or not to use an authentic pea. Rule one seems to be never use real food when you can cut it out of poster board just as well. (This is especially true if your library or classroom has just been newly carpeted, as our library has!) You may try a dried pea, or a cardboard green pea works just fine, thank you!

The advantage of using puppets with this story is that you can really illustrate the humor as the princess thrashes back and forth on the pile of mattresses, atop the small pea. This, of course, proves she is a real princess.

For this story you'll need a princess who gets caught in the rain and seeks shelter; a prince who takes her in and wonders how he can authenticate her princessly status; and a queen mother who dreams up the idea of placing the pea under the pile of mattresses. All those royal family puppets mentioed earlier in this chapter are tailor-made for this. If you don't have them, let it be known among mothers, teachers, staff, and neighbors that you need some dolls. There are always people willing to weed out their toy chests and closets for the cause. Another good source is thrift shops. I've gotten many an item from Goodwill for a dollar or two.

The "mattress" I use came from an Odd Lot discount store—in the form of a package of various colored sponges. A bunch of cut-out brightly colored poster boards taped together would serve just as well.

A musical decision might come up if you're wondering which wedding song to use when the prince finally decides the girl is indeed a real princess: "Here Comes the Bride" or "The Wedding March." First, let's get technical. "Here Comes the Bride" is really Richard Wagner's "Wedding March" from *Lohengrin*; the "Wedding March" (as we call it) is the wedding march from Mendelssohn's *A Midsummer Night's Dream*. Both are usually found on recordings of collections of wedding music.

After the princess's sleepless night atop a sponge-pile mattress, you are ready to bring on the music. If everything is in place, all you need do is hit the play button on your cassette or CD player to fill the room with instantly recognizable bridal music, to the delight of your audience ("Here Comes the Bride" works best). It's an unexpected element and always evokes smiles.

✳ ✳ ✳

"Thumbelina" is another Hans Christian Andersen story which can be enhanced with the same synergistic elements of story, puppets, and music. The many tumultuous adventures of our thumb-sized heroine involve all kinds of delicious characters. A mother frog captures the girl to become a bride for her ugly son. A butterfly and fish rescue Thumbelina from the frog's lily pad and take her to shore. The kindly mouse takes her in from the cold, but insists she marry his friend the mole. Thumbelina finds a "dead" sparrow, which is merely frozen from the cold, and nurses it back to health. Not wanting to marry the mole, she flies away on the bird's back to a land of flowers and eventually marries the angel of the flowers and receives a pair of wings from his little friends. There are more incidents, but I shorten the story for a young audience. Mendelssohn's "Wedding March" can be played for the ceremony at the end.

First I borrowed one of my daughter's dolls to be Thumbelina. Her wings at the end can be cut out of poster board or clipped from a Christmas tree angel. Thumbelina has encounters with frogs, fish, a bird, an angel, and the little people, so I enlisted a volunteer who goes to ten or twenty garage sales each Saturday. She manages to pick up virtual menageries of characters for 25¢ or 50¢ each and donates whatever we need. Also, the casts of such productions can be enhanced by simply asking parents to bring in donations of "weeded" stuffed animals. One librarian in a nearby city suggested that I make a "National Union Catalog" of the bags full of characters I have stored from donations, garage sales, and Goodwill stores.

The puppets and stuffed animals and dolls are an art form in themselves. Basically, when these pop up from behind any improvised or professional puppet stage, they add instant awe to the storytelling. Eyes light up. Mouths fall open. In libraries, regular trips to the programs become priorities with kids and parents. In classrooms and daycare programs, the kids know this is a special treat to be enjoyed. In all places, the underlying goals of creating interest in books, reading, stories, words, and learning are all given a major boost.

✳ ✳ ✳

One final Hans Christian Andersen story to use with puppets and music is "The Emperor's New Clothes." We will need an emperor, two swindlers, a couple of old wise men, one little boy, and various and sundry marches for the parade.

In this one I use a people puppet which I bought at a Puppeteers of America convention a few years ago. It is a handmade man, with removable trousers and shirt. Underneath the clothing is a pink body, or sleeve, for the puppeteer's hand. The effect without the trousers and shirt is perfect for our naked emperor in the story. If you can come up with a similar puppet or doll you're all set.

In this story, the emperor loved to change into new clothes every hour and spent most of his money on them. Two swindlers convince him to give them money to weave new clothes of such a delicate and wonderful nature that only the most discerning people will be able to see them.

The emperor sends a couple of wise old men to check on the progress. Unwilling to admit they may be stupid or incompetent, the wise men return with glowing reports on the new clothing. They even tell the vain emperor that he must wear the new clothes in the big upcoming parade. The swindlers "work" all night to complete the magnificient clothes. On the great day, the emperor puts on the invisible garments, not admitting that he can't see them.

Only when a little boy blurts out, "The emperor has no clothes on!" does the truth become apparent. The emperor bravely keeps his dignified pose until the end of the parade, when he returns to the privacy of his castle and gets dressed.

Any puppets or dolls you have can be used in the processional of townspeople. Stuffed animals can join in. The identities of the cast do not matter as long as they form a parade. Pompous marching music will enhance the point of the story and the atmosphere of a grand royal parade. Elgar's "Pomp and Circumstances March no. 1" is a good choice. Any Sousa marches would also be fine.

✳ ✳ ✳

Puppetry and Hans Christian Andersen

Puppets should be used creatively with storytelling, and not just limited to "puppet shows," which take too much time, too much staff, and too much rehearsal. These "shows" also suffer from our mostly amateurish attempts to do falsetto voices, squeaks, and growls. Librarians, teachers, and parents are terrific storytellers—not Broadway performers! If we can utilize puppets, good music, writing, drawing and art with our storytelling, it's just that much better! Why set limits?

A Sample Musical Story Program
Theme: Hans Christian Andersen Stories
Ages Preschool–9

1. *Musical story*
   Story: "The Real Princess"
   Music: "The Wedding March" from *Lohengrin* (Wagner)
   Musical mood: For a formal marriage ceremony
   Puppets: Princess, prince, queen
   Props: Colored sponges ("mattresses"), pea

2. *Musical story*
   Story: "The Swineherd"
   Music: "The Blue Danube" (Strauss)
   Musical mood: A waltz to illustrate the lovely waltzes played by the magic rattle which the princess wants to buy from the swineherd.
   Puppets: King, princess, prince/swineherd, nightingale, ladies-in-waiting, pigs.
   Props: Disguise (rag fragments) to change prince into swineherd, flower, pot, rattle.

3. *Activity (preschool)*
   Coloring: "The Real Princess" is a story which lends itself to a humorous drawing for young children to color. If you can sketch a sleeping princess on top of simple rectangular mattresses, you can make copies for the children to color the mattresses in different shades (and of course, one green pea).

4. *Art (early elementary)*
   Preschoolers may be more comfortable coloring in a pre-drawn picture, but early elementary children may want to try their hands at drawing their own conceptions of a real princess or prince from scratch.

5. *Creative writing (early elementary)*
   If your group is early elementary age, you might ask them to write (or tell) a story imagining themselves to be a princess or a prince as in the two Andersen tales. You could go over

the basics of short story construction with them: 1) a main character with a situation or problem; 2) supporting characters; 3) actions on the problem; 4) complications; 5) a final resolution (happy or sad for the main character—as the two sample stories illustrate); 6) a theme; 7) a setting; and 8) a time.

Regarding the theme, you could ask older and younger children what they think is the theme or meaning of each of the two stories: "You can't tell too much about a person by what she looks like," and "Fussy people can be a real pain," are two answers I got to this question.

References

Stories:

All of these can be found in virtually any new or old edition of Hans Christian Andersen's fairy tales: "The Emperor's New Clothes"; "The Real Princess"; "The Swineherd"; "Thumbelina."

Record Albums:

Elgar, Edward. "Pomp and Circumstances March no. 1." *Pomp and Circumstance.* Capitol. SP 8620.

Mendelssohn, Felix. "Wedding March" from *A Midsummer Night's Dream. The Hollywood Bowl Wedding Album.* Hollywood Bowl Symphony Orchestra and Roger Wagner Chorale. Capitol SP 8653.

Strauss, Johann. "The Blue Danube Waltz." *A Waltz Spectacular.* Boston Pops. R.C.A. R234007.

Wagner, Richard. "Wedding March" ("Here Comes the Bride") from *Lohengrin. The Hollywood Bowl Wedding Album.* Hollywood Bowl Symphony Orchestra and Roger Wagner Chorale. Capitol SP 8653.

Compact Disc:

Mendelssohn, Felix. "Wedding March" from *A Midsummer Night's Dream*. Boston Symphony Orchestra. R.C.A. 60910–2.

3
Viva, Vivaldi!

In 1991, a great musical milestone passed virtually unnoticed. That year marked the 250th anniversary of the death of the great Italian composer Antonio Vivaldi. There had been quite a bit of attention paid to the fact that 1991 was the 200th anniversary of Mozart's death. Both men of genius were unceremoniously laid to rest in paupers' graves. Mozart's 200th gave rise to festivals, concerts, posters, newly recorded releases, radio and television specials—but Vivaldi's 250th anniversary seems to have drawn about as much attention as his funeral. You would think that someone who had such a major influence on such composers as Johann Sebastian Bach would get a little attention from our modern-day society on such an anniversary!

Vivaldi (1678–1741) wrote about 500 concertos for almost every instrument known in his time: violins, oboes, mandolins, flutes, piccolos, and so on. They are so rich in mood, atmosphere, and pace that it's easy to devote an entire chapter to matching Vivaldi's music with children's stories.

Marc Pincherle's book, *Vivaldi, Genius of the Baroque*, offers a fascinating historical description which may explain why Vivaldi's music is especially good for children's programs. Although he was known far and wide as "The Red Priest," or *Prete Rosso*, Vivaldi's asthma prevented him from saying Mass, and he therefore concentrated on his music. In 1703 Vivaldi became a violin teacher at a Venetian girls' orphanage (the Osperdale della Pietà,) housing as many as 6,000 girls and young women. He became the composer, the buyer of instruments, the teacher, the conductor, and the maestro who took the girls on concert tours all over Europe for the next forty years. Perhaps his work with these young orphans and abandoned girls explains why his music seems especially appropriate for combining with children's stories. Just from the section titles of his well-known work, *The Four Seasons* — "Spring," "Summer," "Fall," and "Winter" — you can see that it holds many possibilities for tie-ins with children's books.

✵ ✵ ✵

One of the genuine thrills I had from writing my book *Musical Story Hours* was having storyteller Caroline Feller Bauer tell me that she loved it. So one of the thrills of this sequel is to set two of her books to the music of *The Four Seasons*. Caroline Bauer has written many books herself; has lectured in every state in the country; has told stories for years on her own television show; and has taught library science and made storytelling videos. Let's start with one of her books which obviously says a great deal about Ms. Bauer's lifestyle: *My Mom Travels a Lot*.

This picture book is a real charmer, dedicated to Ms. Bauer's daughter Hilary and told from a young girl's point of view. This child tells us the good things and the bad things about her mom's frequent travels: she gets to go to the airport quite a bit, for instance, but then there's only one fatherly good night kiss.

In keeping with the travel theme, I thought of trying the joyous, bouncy melody of the third movement in the "Spring" section (*Allegro*) of *The Four Seasons*. The music gives the impression of walking through a beautiful new spring day, or of skipping or driving or flying — in other words, of moving around. It is an ideal companion to the travel theme of this story.

✵ ✵ ✵

Another of Caroline Bauer's picture books is *The Midnight Snowman*. This story captures the excitement of children over a late night snowfall in a town where it rains, but hardly ever snows. Because snow is so rare, the children are allowed to stay up past their usual bedtimes, go outside, and build a snowman. They are delighted with the opportunity.

Viva, Vivaldi!

I've gone over the "Winter" section of *The Four Seasons* to find a musical match-up for this story. Although much of the winter music is too stormy to fit, the second movement, the *Largo*, has a soft melody backed up by continually-plucked violin strings, evocative of lightly falling snow.

✳ ✳ ✳

In contrast to the gentle snowfall, Berta and Elmer Hader's Caldecott Award book, *The Big Snow*, has a fiercer snowstorm. The finale of Vivaldi's "Winter" section makes a more appropriate backdrop for this story. You may need to turn your stereo or tape player down as you read this one, since the music is louder.

✳ ✳ ✳

A cheerful story about an elf who, like Vivaldi, plays the violin, is Don Madden's *Lemonade Serenade*. This goes well with an equally cheerful "Concerto in C major for Violin, Two String Choirs and Two Harpsichords" by Vivaldi. The music need not start until the elf begins to fiddle.

Madden's book follows Emalina Twig, who strolls through her non-formal formal garden every morning telling her plants that she loves them. Her best friend is a young boy, Woodrow Worthington, who has cookies and lemonade with her every afternoon by the birdbath.

A horrible and strange noise comes from behind the bushes one day, and Woodrow bravely investigates. Could it be lions? Tigers? A space ship? Woodrow discovers that it is merely an elf making noise on his boombamaphone, a contraption made from a bathtub, row boat, and hoses.

The ever-pleasant Miss Twig sets out the next day to buy a gift violin for this musically-inclined little character. The good-natured rich lady and the boy invite the elf to join them on a regular basis and perform "lemonade serenades" on his violin at daily concerts in the garden.

This story could lend itself to some puppet involvement, especially in the garden. Lions, tigers, etc., can pop up from the bush branches and artifical flowers, while the lead characters sip lemonade on stage behind the storyteller.

For an after-story art activity you could pass out pictures of the elf (drawn and photocopied ahead of time), for the younger children to color while the violin concerto plays all the way through. It makes a nice transition to the activity as well as an appropriate touch in the story itself.

＊ ＊ ＊

So What? is the intriguing and philosophical title of author Miriam Cohen's 1982 picture book. This story describes the misadventures of a first grader name Jim. Everybody else in the schoolyard can hang upside down on the jungle gym without holding on. Jim cannot. He feels bad about it, and says so to Elinor, the new girl from Chicago. So he holds on with his hands— "So what?" she encourages him—while shooting basketballs through a hoop.

Jim hopes to become more popular, so he starts a club. He even invents a secret "Hello" greeting involving elaborate head shakes. Other kids get dizzy from all the shaking and quit his club. "So what?" the philosophical Elinor reassures Jim.

Further damage is done to the boy's ego when the students are measured for height by the school nurse. Jim is found to be the shortest at 3'9". Not by much, but it's still upsetting. "So what?" Elinor repeats.

The teacher is critical of Jim's square dancing skills, and she even forgets his name. "So what?" the girl shrugs, but Jim can't get over any of this.

Suddenly Elinor is gone. Her family has moved back to Chicago.

One day Jim is thinking of all his troubles while he hangs upside down on the jungle gym. He says, "So what?" just like Elinor and—for the first time—finds the courage to let go.

Looking for a muscial match for this story, I wanted something light and playful that suggested an interplay between two close pals. I chose the opening movement from Vivaldi's sparkling "Concerto in G Major for Two Mandolins" from the cas-

sette, *Concertos for Diverse Instruments*. The back and forth
cheery and supportive interplay between the two mandolins was
just right. The musical mood is light and bouncy, as are Jim's
problems. We're not dealing with deep psychology here!

✳ ✳ ✳

Another Vivaldi cassette which is a delight is *Vivaldi's Lute
and Mandolin Concerto*, played by the Württemberg Chamber
Orchestra. One of the real gems in this collection is the "Trio in
G Minor for Lute, Strings and Continuo." The first movement
(*Andante Molto*) and the third (*Allegro*) both feature the rapid
staccato pluckings of the lute. If you let your imagination go, you
can picture short-legged creatures scurrying along the ground in
zig-zag fashion.

The musical imagery of this cheerful piece fits perfectly with
a story such as Mirra Ginsburg's *The Chick and the Duckling*,
translated from the Russian of V. Suteyev.

In this story we first meet the two principal characters as
they hatch from their respective eggs. The duckling decides to
take a walk, and the impressionable chick does the same. The
duckling then announces he will search for worms. The chick
joins in the hunt. The duckling tries and succeeds in catching a
butterfly, as does the copycat chick. The little duck then goes for
a swim.

The chick decides to take a swim, too, and dives right in, but
sinks to the bottom. The duckling rescues the chick and announces that he's going back for another swim. This time the
chick asserts his independence. "Not me," he says with finality.

The lesson about being true to your nature is not lost on the
children, who love the musical match-up here.

✳ ✳ ✳

Henry and Mudge Get the Cold Shivers by Cynthia Rylant
will give you a complete change of pace. While the story of the
duckling and chick was fast-paced throughout, in this one the
main characters both get sick and can hardly move.

When the boy Henry gets sick, his big dog Mudge profits

from it. Mom and Dad bring popsicles, comic books, and crackers. Mudge gets to eat the crackers because Henry doesn't feel up to nibbling.

One day Mudge himself can only look up from the floor and wag his tail a little at Henry. Mudge is indeed in sorry shape, and Henry and his family get Mudge to a veterinarian. Henry is left in the waiting room, where he worries if Mudge knows how to say "Ah," and if the dog will be all right. The veterinarian gives Henry cold medicine for Mudge, and prescribes plenty of rest. She also tells Henry not to kiss the dog until he's better!

Henry sets up a recovery area in the family living room, complete with a blanket, pillow, some dirty socks, a stuffed moose, a baseball mitt, and a rubber hamburger. The family brings crackers.

The following day sees Mudge recover, eat some crackers, and give Henry a big kiss. All ends happily.

The versatile Vivaldi has a "Concerto in C Major for Mandolin and Strings," second movement (*Largo*), which goes very well with this story. This *Largo* is a slow, melodious section which mirrors the pace at which both characters move when they become ill. This particular piece of music is also very affectionate. I've even heard it used in a movie backing up a romantic scene in a gondola. In the case of Henry and Mudge, the tone is not what you'd call romantic (despite all the kissing) but the extremely sweet music works just as well.

✳ ✳ ✳

We've already seen quite a range of use for these Vivaldi concertos. Let's try another change of pace here. Let's take a purely comical story and see if our Italian master can stick with us.

Steven Kellogg's 1981 book, *A Rose for Pinkerton*, concerns a huge dog much like Mudge in the previous book. Pinkerton is a Great Dane who is lonely. The family thinks one Great Dane is enough, so rather than buy a puppy to keep the dog company they buy a kitten named Rose.

Rose promptly tries to scratch the dog's face, eats his food, and takes over his personal spot of sunshine on the floor.

Later in the story there is a pet show, which features a poodle parade. Rose wants to be a poodle, so she breaks away and joins in. The judge screams, and the poodles chase the cat—right toward the Castle of Kittens. The castle, with Pinkerton in it, topples over. The sight of the huge dog causes the poodles to fall into a faint. At first people want to arrest Pinkerton, but they decide instead that he is a hero for saving the kittens.

There are other books about Pinkerton, as there are in the Henry and Mudge series. Pinkerton is always madcap and zany, and deserves some humorous background music. You might think we'd have to leave the classical concertos of Vivaldi to find something appropriate, but it is not so.

The bassoon is a musical instrument which has a humorous sound—not at all noble like a trumpet. Vivaldi wrote a "Concerto in G Minor for Bassoon" (again, on the *Concertos for Diverse Instruments* tape). The first movement, *Presto*, is probably the best to use for comic background effect because of its general peppiness and the comically odd sound of the bassoon. The third movements, *Allegro*, can be used in the same way, perhaps with a different funny story.

As far as puppets go, one of our mothers donated a three-foot-tall stuffed dog which we use for Pinkerton and Mudge or any other "large dog" story. We have a normal array of humans (children and adults), kittens, cats, etc., in either puppet or stuffed animal form, to act out some of the major events of the two stories, silently, as I read the story, paraphrasing as I show the illustrations, and the music is played backstage.

✳ ✳ ✳

Michael Gay, a French writer from Paris, is an accomplished musician and composer himself. He might enjoy knowing that someone matched his picture book, *The Little Airplane*, with the opening movement of Vivaldi's "Piccolo Concerto in C Major." Piccolo music—especially if it's fast -tends to give the impression of birds or flight. I've used the opening movement with the airplane book and the finale with a bird book.

The Little Airplane is a simple picture book, good to use with preschoolers. It is a beautiful day and the sky is bright blue when the little airplane takes off, leaving smoke trails behind. When it's too cold up high, the plane dives lower. When it's in the mood, the plane turns over and over in big, looping somersaults. When it feels peppy, it scoots past the birds. When it feels tired, it rests on a cloud. Finally when the sun goes down, the little airplane returns to its house on the ground.

With a toy airplane on a long wire, (or on a coat hanger pulled apart), and a few bird puppets or stuffed birds on wires, you can add a bit of visual effect from a puppet stage behind you while you read the story and show the illustrations. The opening of the "Piccolo Concerto" adds more to that feeling of flight.

✳ ✳ ✳

Let's try the third section of the concerto with John Hamberger's bird book, *The Wish*. In this book, the identity of the main character remains hidden until the end. (I'll tell you — it's a penguin!) This penguin wishes that he were another kind of bird. If that could only be, he would fly through the sky, build a nest in the trees, and soar with the other birds. He could stretch out his wings, turn spirals in the clouds, and weave in and out of the many stars, between the plentiful trees, or through the gently falling drops of rain. He could perch in a tree full of cherry blossoms. He could dance with the ocean waves, the penguin thinks. Then he realizes he can do that anyway. In fact, he's doing it!

Suddenly his attitude improves. He now thinks of all the wonderful things a penguin can do which other birds cannot do. He can dive underwater like a fish. He can swim. He can leap out of the water like a dolphin. Being a penguin (or being oneself) is not such a bad thing after all.

A bird on a wire and a penguin puppet are nice additions for the puppet stage behind the storyteller. You need to be careful always to keep the music in the background, and the storyteller dominant in this type of program.

✳ ✳ ✳

It's truly a shame that so little of the world's attention went to the 250th anniversary of Vivaldi's passing. If one good thing happens as a result of this book, I hope it includes a widespread revival of interest among children's librarians and teachers in the miraculous music of the Red Priest! Viva, Vivaldi!

A Sample Musical Story Hour
Theme: Dogs
Ages 4–8

1. *Participation songs*

   "How Much Is That Doggie in the Window?" Children can bark. Dog puppet can romp.

   "This Old Man" (or, "Knick, Knack, Paddy Whack"). Children can give cut-out bones to the dog puppet at each "Give a dog a bone" line.

2. *Musical story*

   Story: *Henry and Mudge Get the Cold Shivers* (Cynthia Rylant)

   Music: "Concerto in C Major for Mandolin and Strings" (Vivaldi)

   Musical mood: Affectionate; weary (both characters are ill in this story)

3. *Musical story*

   Story: *The Midnight Snowman* (Carolyn Bauer)

   Music: "Winter" section (*Largo*) from *The Four Seasons* (Vivaldi)

   Musical mood: Comical, off-beat

4. *Activity*

   Coloring with crayons. Sketch and photocopy a picture of a snowman, with snow falling around him, dressed in a hat and scarf, for all to color and take home.

5. *Arts activities*

   Art appreciation:

   Since we used parts of *The Four Seasons* with Caroline Bauer's stories, let's use the same music as a starting point for looking at some famous art works on the seasons. There is so much to choose from! For example,

   Winter: Currier and Ives paintings

   Grandma Moses's *The First Skating*

   Summer: Seurat's pointillist masterpiece, *Sunday Afternoon at the Grande Jatte*

Fall: Grandma Moses's *The Falling Leaves*
Spring: Fragonard's *The Swing*

The following activities are for older children, ages 9 to 12, during school age library story hours or class visits, or used by teachers in class.

Drawing:

Seeing Fragonard's young woman on a swing in a garden of flowers and trees would certainly evoke feelings of spring. The autumn and winter scenes of Anna Mary Robertson (Grandma) Moses certainly capture those seasonal moods. Seurat's Sunday strollers evoke a leisurely summer's day. What memories can the children capture on paper from their own experiences tied in with the seasons?

6. *Creative writing*

The four seasons theme is ideal for introducing older children to poetry.

A brief definition and example of the basic meters gives children a fun assortment of creative writing possibilities to play with:

Meter	Emphasis	Example
Iambic	no accent, accent	Laverne (La-VERNE)
Trochaic	accent, no accent	Shirley (SHIR-ley)
Dactyl	accent, 2 no accents	Dorothy (DO-ro-thy)
Anapest	2 no accents, accent	Antoinette (An-toi-NETTE)
Amphibrach	no accent, accent, no accent	Louisa (Lou-I-sa)

The children can experiment with writing or sounding out some of these meters using familiar words or names. It is not important that they know the formal name of each; only that language can form patterns of sound, and these patterns can be used in poetry. They might try making up their own poems about the four seasons using one of the meters, such as iambic. For example:

The leaves fell down   (the LEAVES / fell DOWN)
Onto the ground   (on-TO / the GROUND)

Another fun way to explore simple metrics is to use famous poems and ask the children to guess. An example is Clement Moore's "The Night Before Christmas":

'Twas the NIGHT before CHRISTmas
And ALL through the HOUSE . . .

You're right! Anapests!

References

Books:

Bauer, Caroline Feller. *Handbook for Storytellers.* American Library Association, 1977.
————. *The Midnight Snowman.* Atheneum, 1987.
————. *My Mom Travels a Lot.* Puffin Books, 1985.
————. *This Way to Books.* H. W. Wilson, 1983.
Cohen, Miriam. *So What?* Greenwillow, 1982.
Gay, Michael. *The Little Airplane.* Macmillan, 1983.
Ginsburg, Mirra. *The Chick and the Duckling.* Macmillan, 1972.
Hader, Berta and Elmer. *The Big Snow.* Macmillan, 1976.
Hamberger, John. *The Wish.* W. W. Norton, 1967.
Kellogg, Steven. *A Rose for Pinkerton.* Dial, 1981.
Madden, Don. *Lemonade Serenade — or — the Thing in the Garden.* Albert Whitman, 1966.
Pincherle, Marc. *Vivaldi, Genius of the Baroque.* W. W. Norton, 1957.
Rylant, Cynthia. *Henry and Mudge Get the Cold Shivers.* Bradbury, 1989.

Cassettes:

Vivaldi, Antonio. *The Four Seasons.* "Winter" (second movement, *Largo*); "Spring" (third movement, *Allegro*). Madacy. MKC 1818.

————. "Concerto in C for Violin, Two String Choirs, and Two Harpsichords"; "Concerto in G Major for Two Mandolins"; "Concerto in G Minor for Bassoon"; "Piccolo Concerto in C Major." *Vivaldi Concertos for Diverse Instruments.* The Bach Guild. Historical Anthology of Music. Vanguard. CHM 16.

————. "Concerto in C Major for Mandolin and String Orchestra"; "Trio in G for Violin, Lute and Continuo." *Vivaldi's Lute and Mandolin Concertos.* Württemberg Chamber Orchestra. Vox/Turnabout. CT 2128.

————. *Guitar Concertos.* Los Romeros. Philips. 426 076–4.

Compact Disc:

Vivaldi, Antonio. *The Four Seasons.* "Winter" (second movement, *Largo*); "Spring" (third movement, *Allegro*). Leopold Stowkowski. New Philharmonic Orchestra. London. 433–680–2.

4

Papa Bach
and Children's Stories

I suppose the idea of matching a composer like Bach with children's stories will strike some people as bizarre—but indeed it is not. Certainly anybody who had twenty children himself ought to be given some consideration for this type of thing! Here is just a small segment of Bach's voluminous musical output—mostly his six Brandenburg Concertos—with suggestions for using them with children's stories.

The six Brandenburg Concertos are like the children in most families: each is distinctly different from the others. The third is exclusively strings, while the second features trumpets, the fifth a harpsichord, and the fourth, flutes. The first is more an ensemble piece, and the sixth spotlights strings in a more traditional three-movement form.

*** *** ***

Arnold Lobel's *Frog and Toad Are Friends* is a perennial favorite of preschoolers. The humorous adventures of the two friends take the form of a series of rollicking anecdotal stories.

Frog calls to the sleepy Toad to wake up and start the spring season. Toad replies that he's not there and goes back to bed. Eventually awake, Toad later tries to think of a story to tell his sick friend, Frog. Toad stands on his head to try to think of one, to no avail. He tries pouring water on his face, but still no story comes to mind. He bangs his head on the wall, but even this does not jog his memory. Feeling ill from the head-banging, Toad crawls back into bed himself. Frog feels better, so *he* gets up and tells a story to Toad.

As time goes on, the friends are up and about and ready for a swim in the pond. Frog doesn't wear a bathing suit, but Toad does—and a rather silly one at that. Toad shoos a turtle away, afraid he will look at Toad's striped suit and laugh. Naturally, the word spreads and everyone comes for a look—the snake, two dragonflies, a mouse, a lizard. They tell Toad that he does indeed look funny. He summons up his dignity and says, "Of course I do" and leaves for home.

These quiet and good-natured stories follow one after the other, and I found a perfectly delightful piece of good-natured romping music to go along with the friends. Bach's masterful "Brandenburg Concerto no. 3" is a two-movement string piece that travels along at a briskly moderate pace in its opening *Alle Breve* movement. I'd have to say this may well be my one favorite piece of music. It is charming and upbeat and full of life—a perfect mood piece for Frog and Toad.

An interesting tie-in with a work of art on the theme of animals as friends is Edward Hicks's famous painting, *The Peaceable Kingdom* (1830). This American Quaker primitive artist painted a state of nature where no hatred exists. Various large and potentially dangerous animals are seen lying down peacefully together in an Eden-like setting, along with three humans as well. This painting hangs today in New York's Metropolitan Museum of Art, and it can be found reproduced in Newsweek's "Great Museums of the World" book series, in the *Metropolitan Museum of Art* volume edited by Lucia Ragghianti. Another good painting to show is Henri Rousseau's *Sleeping Gypsy*. You can ask, "Does the lion sniffing the gypsy look friendly—or hungry?" "What makes you think the lion is glad to see the gypsy—or makes you think he sees a good meal?"

As a project for the kids themselves, you may ask them to make a drawing of their own best friends and tell about what things they do together, like Frog and Toad.

✳ ✳ ✳

The second movement of this "Brandenburg Concerto no. 3" is also a pure string piece, only here the tempo goes from moderate to fast—*Allegro*. It is also charming, but could use a faster-paced story for this piece of music. How about the comical adventures of a young duck learning to fly? Abigail Pizer's *Percy the Duck* shows us a lovable duck at Nettlepatch Farm who goes through all kinds of efforts to learn to fly like the older ducks.

Percy runs as fast as he can, tries to take off—and crashes into an old pile of tires. He jumps off a barn roof and lands ignominiously in the pigs' water trough. From the heights of a bale of straw he dives into the depths of a mud puddle. Thinking he's too heavy, he diets to become more aerodynamic. Nothing works except the passage of time. When Percy is old enough to fly, he flies—proudly and happily—and the boisterous second movement of the Bach piece makes a great action-packed background for his flighty adventure.

✳ ✳ ✳

Let's try Bach in a different mood. If anyone enjoyed the movie, *Children of a Lesser God*, starring William Hurt and Marlee Matlin, you may recall the Bach music that Hurt's character, James Leeds, listened to for relaxation and pleasure. This poignant and lovely piece in the film was Bach's "Concerto for Two Violins"—the second movement (*Largo*).

There's a perfect classic bedtime story for such sleepy and mesmerizing music: *Bedtime for Frances*, Russell Hoban's lovable picture book. Frances does everything possible to stall off the inevitable bedtime. She wants a glass of milk, a piggyback ride, a teddy bear, a doll, a kiss, another kiss, a song, a search for possible giants and bugs. . . . Finally a mention of a possible spanking dispels all such tactics and the idea of a nice long slumber begins to have immediate appeal.

Bach and the restful bed make a very nice combination in this instance.

Since Frances wanted her doll in bed, I think another famous girl and doll would be interesting to show with the story. Norman Rockwell's beloved *Doctor and Doll* from 1923 shows the doctor patiently and cheerfully applying the stethoscope to the chest of a girl's doll. He is pretending to listen attentively. This painting can be found in *Norman Rockwell's America*, edited by Christopher Finch.

An art project could be to have children draw a picture of themselves in bed, or at play with their own favorite doll, toy, or stuffed animal. They could also tell the other kids why they chose their particular favorites, or make up reasons—like Frances—why they just *can't* go to bed. The storyteller could pretend to be a parent sternly saying, "Go to bed!" while the kids could offer creative excuses for staying up. This makes a cute game and a dialogue, full of humor and not a little mischief!

✳ ✳ ✳

Let's take a look at a more recent book now, published thirty years after *Bedtime for Frances*, giving us another little character staving off bedtime. James Sage's book *To Sleep* shows us a mother trying to get her boy to go to sleep at the end of the day. Where is this mythical end of the day, the child wants to know. The mother imaginatively explains that it is beyond the pillow and the bed and the room. At this point, the bed takes off through the window, as the boy continues to ask what is beyond the room. Mother, child, and bed fly over the path that leads to town. What's beyond there? Well, there's the countryside, the city, the sea, the mountains . . . the stars . . . dreams. . . .

As with Frances, the parent finally comes down to earth and resolves the situation. Dreams come from your head, she explains, which is on your pillow, in your bed, where you are safe and warm. (In other words, go to sleep now!)

Bach's "Brandenburg Concerto no. 4," as I mentioned, features flutes. The flighty third movement, *Presto*, aptly fits the adventures of this child and mother on their flying bed. This sky-ride flute music and story make a very effective match up, as both are fast and airy and highly imaginative.

✳ ✳ ✳

Let's take a look now at another book featuring a flying

bed—Chris Van Allsburg's environmental picture book, *Just a Dream.* While *Bedtime for Frances* and *To Sleep* are fine for pre-schoolers and early elementary children up to second or third grade, *Just a Dream* is more specifically for grades one through three, in library or school settings.

In this contemporary tale, young Walter comes out of the bakery with a jelly doughnut and carelessly throws the empty bag toward a fire hydrant, littering the street. He goes home and makes fun of Rose, the neighbor girl, who is watering the tree she received for her birthday.

When he takes out the trash that evening, he is supposed to sort the bottles, cans, and miscellaneous items, but recycling is not on his mind. He lumps everything together.

That night his careless ways come back to haunt him. He dreams that his bed flies off to a trash dump, and then to a sickening collection of huge active smokestacks. The bed then takes him to a place where men are chopping down trees, to be made into toothpicks. The bed travels on to the beautiful mountains, but soon a giant hotel appears, to mar the natural beauty. Expressways fill the sky and car horns blare.

The bed flies on, to the Grand Canyon, where the view is obscured by smog. A guide tries to sell Walter postcards of the canyon on a clear day.

When Walter awakens, he jumps to mend his wicked ways. He runs back to pick up his jelly doughnut bag, sorts the trash, and even plants a tree. He sees into a future when his tree and Rose's tree are grown and providing a lovely sight and shade in their yards.

This is a great story for Earth Day, April 22, and certainly a thought-provoking one. An interesting twist is the presence of a pet white cat, looking trustingly at Walter throughout the story. The boy does turn out to be worthy of this wordless trust.

Bach can be useful here, too, in creating a mood. The final *Allegro* movement of his "Brandenburg Concerto no. 5" features an agitated harpsichord movement that sets a tone for the agitated bed ride through a very upsetting and polluted world. Even the tinny sound of the harpsichord itself adds to the feeling of this frenetic trip. You might want to switch to something nicer and more serene for the ending. How about Bach's own "Sheep Shall Safely Graze," which sounds exactly like its title! This might be a great chance to ask the kids why they think one piece of music can make them feel jumpy, and another, peaceful. You can point out the difference between an agitated *Allegro* (especially on a harpsichord, that early, tinny version of the piano) and a calm, serene, *Largo*.

✳ ✳ ✳

Bach's most recognizable piece is a cheerful little tune which is often heard on the radio, especially at Christmas, on classical and easy-listening stations, on department store muzak, on church bells—everywhere. Most people remember it from somewhere, but have no idea that it is a hymn, with the serious title of "Jesu, Joy of Man's Desiring." This infectious, melodious, and even hummable Bach piece can be used with any joyful, light, and upbeat story. I've done just that, many times; the latest is with Judith Viorst's comical portrait of a girl who is wholly determined to get her ears pierced (someday, soon). This picture book is *Earrings*, and the girl spends the entire book coming up with arguments to convince her parents that she is *not* too young to have her ears pierced; that she does *not* want to wait until she's 20, 40, 80, or 100 to do it; that she is the *only* girl in the solar system without pierced ears; and that the lovely jewelry she would wear would even improve her posture!

The repetitive nature of the Bach tune matches the repetitive, nonstop efforts of this girl to get her way. Although she is indeed overbearing, the portrait is good-natured and cheerful. Let it be pointed out, also, that despite the book full of reasons thrown at her "old-fashioned" parents, the girl still does *not* have pierced ears at the end. Of course, there may well be a sequel, but as of this writing the parents have had the final word and the girl must wait a couple of years!

It's fun to show Egyptian earrings, the earliest dating from around 1500 B.C., and point out just how many centuries these baubles have been popular. Two elaborate ones from King Tut's time are pictured in color in the Metropolitan Museum of Art's *Treasures of Tutankhamun.* A sense of history can be gleaned from these treasures, and the mummies are a near-guaranteed hit!

This story has some other very interesting counterparts which you could bring in from the world of art and art history. In modern times, two of the most famous depictions of earrings appear in Degas's *A Woman with Chrysanthemums* (1865) and Manet's *Boating* (1882), which shows a nicely dressed lady out rowing with her gentleman friend.

Both paintings are hanging today in New York's Metropolitan Museum of Art and are reproduced in the Newsweek museum book series, "Great Museums of the World," in the *Metropolitan Museum* volume.

However, it is fascinating to follow the human love of earrings much farther back in time. Newsweek has a volume on *The Museum of Fine Arts, Boston* edited by Cavallo et al., which shows *The Bodhisattva's Bath in the Niranjana River,* from first-century India, a sculpture which also depicts people with prominent earrings. The same book shows us *Amithaba with Acolytes,* a twelfth-century gouache painting on cloth from Nepal, featuring circular green-and-yellow earrings on the principal figure. Ask the children why they think people wear earrings, and then ask if they think they could convince their parents to let them have earrings too. (In some communities the children will have had earrings from infancy, so you can admire the many different ones they wear.)

✳ ✳ ✳

Another word about "Jesu, Joy of Man's Desiring" by Bach. The repetitive nature of the tune and its march-like beat make it appropriate for a story about a parade as well, such as Ezra Jack Keats's *The Pet Show.* In this classic, Archie can't find his cat to enter into the local pet show. There's a dog, a mouse, a bird, ants, and a goldfish, but no cat. Archie innovatively brings a jar with a "germ" inside, and wins a prize anyhow. An old lady finds his cat and she gets a prize, too. The cheerfulness and humor of this story, and its parade theme, match up well with "Jesu, Joy of Man's Desiring."

✳ ✳ ✳

Now let's look to Bach for (as comedian Jackie Gleason used to say) "a little travelin' music." We need such music to go with a much-traveled teddy bear in Richard Galbraith's picture book, *Reuben Runs Away.*

The story focuses on a teddy bear who lives with a young girl, Anna, plus her family and her dog, Raffles. Anna doesn't really treat her bear with the proper respect: she hangs him up by his ears on the clothesline, for instance. She also has a nasty habit of strapping him into a toy parachute and dropping him out of a tall tree. On top of this, Raffles chews on the poor bear, too.

Enough is enough. The bear runs away. Unfortunately, however, the hotel does not admit teddy bears, so Reuben sleeps in a garbage can, dreaming of Anna. An old lady finds him and sells him to an old man who owns a second-hand shop. Another elderly man spots the bear and buys him for his granddaughter, who just happens to be Anna. The girl's treatment of the bear markedly improves after this absence—except for her fondness for that parachute. . . .

Bach's "Brandenburg Concerto no. 6," much like the third in its concentration on stringed instruments, starts out with a very peppy first movement (*Alle Breva*), which fits very well with the travels and adventures of the bear.

✳ ✳ ✳

Lost in all this talk about creating moods and atmospheres is another consideration. The music kids are exposed to—or bombarded with—today is generally the boom box-amplified noise that goes through the walls of houses a block away. It booms out of car radios, virtually every store in every mall, the length and breadth of every public beach and park—like the common cold, there's no escape. It is a rare and enriching experience for kids to come into a library or classroom, listen to a good story, and have the mood enhanced by the music of Bach. Stop and think how often many of these children will ever have such an opportunity as they grow up!

A book which returns us to an older way of life is *At Taylor's Place* by Sharon Denslow. This is a look into a shop where a man makes weathervanes, whirligigs, bird boxes, and bird feeders. A little girl named Tory carves miniature baskets out of peach pits, adding her own little apprentice touch to the old man's master creations.

There is plenty of atmosphere in the lovely illustrations in this book: wood shavings and hot chocolate and a crackling fire. The portrait is based on the author's own uncle and his workshop, and the atmosphere is totally convincing. Bach's "Brandenburg Concerto no. 6" offers a tender second movement (*Adagio*), and the predominant strings weave a poignant background for this obviously affectionate story.

Let's return to Norman Rockwell for a counterpart in art which also looks back at a more gentle and less complicated era. Rockwell's *The Horseshoe Forging Contest* from Finch's *Norman Rockwell's America* takes us back to a time and place, as the book does, when there was more emphasis on real crafts and real skills. There is a nostalgic portrait in both the book and in the painting, and we glimpse an older way of life.

✳ ✳ ✳

Finally, I hope you won't be so reluctant at this point to include such an imposing figure as J.S. Bach into your story programs for young children. Don't be intimidated. After all, twenty little Bachs called him Papa!

A Sample Arts-Related Story Hour Program
Theme: Growing Up
Ages 4–8

1. *Participation song*

   "I Won't Grow Up" (from the musical of *Peter Pan*). Say that the next two stories are about a young duck and a young girl who both *wanted* to grow up—at least enough to stay up as late as they chose and to wear what they wanted to wear. You could ask the kids if *they* think it's better to grow up or stay put!

2. *Musical story*

   Story: *Bedtime for Frances* (Russell Hoban)

   Music: *Largo* from "Concerto for Two Violins" (Bach)

   Musical mood: Sleepy, wistful, tender.

   Puppets and props: All you need is a duck (puppet or stuffed) plus various props for attempted take-off.

   Art: *Doctor and Doll* (Rockwell)

   Activity: "Tell me about your favorite stuffed animal or doll. What's its name? What do you do together?"

3. *Musical story*

   Story: *Earrings* (Judith Viorst)

   Music: "Jesu, Joy of Man's Desiring" (Bach)

   Musical mood: Serious but full of joy and life. The good-natured fun of this tongue-in-cheek story of the girl's repeated and unending demands for earrings is reflected in the cheerfully oft-repeated melody.

   Art: *A Woman with Chrysanthemums* (Degas)

       Boating (Manet)

       The Bodhisattva's Bath (India)

       Amithaba with Acolytes (Nepal)

   Art Project: Draw yourself with earrings, rings, or jewelry of your imagination.

   Activity: Coloring. Draw a picture of a girl with very gaudy earrings for the children to color.

References

Books:

Cavallo, Adolpho, et al., eds. *The Museum of Fine Arts, Boston.* Great Museums of the World. Newsweek, 1972.

Denslow, Sharon. *At Taylor's Place.* Bradbury Press, 1990.

Finch, Christopher. *Norman Rockwell's America.* Reader's Digest/Harry N. Abrams Co., 1975.

Galbraith, Richard. *Reuben Runs Away.* Orchard Books, 1987.

Hoban, Russell. *Bedtime for Frances.* Harper and Row, 1960.

Keats, Ezra Jack. *Pet Show.* Macmillan, 1972.

Lobel, Arnold. *Frog and Toad Are Friends.* Harper and Row, 1970.

Metropolitan Museum of Art. *Treasures of Tutankhamun.* Metropolitan Museum of Art, 1976.

Pizer, Abigail. *Percy the Duck.* Carolrhoda, 1989.

Ragghianti, Lucia. *The Metropolitan Museum of Art.* Great Museums of the World. Newsweek, 1978.

Sage, James. *To Sleep.* Margaret McElderry Books, 1990.

Van Allsburg, Chris. *Just a Dream.* Houghton Mifflin, 1990.

Viorst, Judith, *Earrings.* Atheneum, 1990.

Compact Discs:

Bach, Johann Sebastian. "Brandenburg Concerto no. 3," first movement (*Alle Breve*) and second movement (*Allegro*). *Bach.* Brandenburg *Concertos.* Academy of Ancient Music. Decca. 414 187–2.

———. "Brandenburg Concerto no. 4," third movement (*Presto*). *Ibid.*

———. "Brandenburg Concerto no. 5," third movement (*Allegro*). *Ibid.*

———. "Brandenburg Concerto no. 6," first movement (*Alle Breve*) and second movement (*Adagio*). *Ibid.*

Cassettes:

Bach, Johann Sebastian. "Concerto for Two Violins in D Minor." *Bach. Violin Concerti.* 412 496–4.

———. "Sheep Shall Safely Graze." *Bach's Greatest.* Golden Classics. GC 27105.

———. "Jesu, Joy of Man's Desiring." *Ibid.*

5

Mischievous Characters

Let's take a look at how one thing can lead to another in using stories, puppets, music, art, drawing, writing and other arts. Let's also look at some naughty characters in children's books.

I want to start with a story familiar to everyone: *Peter Rabbit* by Beatrix Potter. The most famous prop in the story is, of course, the watering can. Bring one into your story hour, add a stuffed rabbit, and you can bring the story right off the page for your kids. But the watering can alone offers myriad chances to venture off into all kinds of arts projects, as you will see.

In the story, Peter's mother tells him not to venture into Mr. McGregor's garden, but, naturally, he goes anyway. His siblings, Flopsy, Mopsy, and Cottontail all obey their mother, but Peter does no such thing. He goes into the garden, eats some lettuce, beans, and radishes, and is soon spotted and chased by Mr. McGregor. Peter hides in the watering can until he can escape under the gate. (For a tiny, scared rabbit, I recommended delicate rhythmic music like Boccherini's "Minuet.")

At this point in the story, you can switch from storyteller to part-time art teacher. Begin by finding a reproduction of the art world's most famous watering bucket, in Renoir's *Girl with a Watering Can*. Here at the North Miami Public Library we have a framed art print in our circulating collection, which I've shown to kids on occasion at the story hour. Many libraries have these circulating art collections, but the picture is also reproduced in any number of art books.

If you look closely at the watering can in Beatrix Potter's illustration, you will see seven holes in its sprinkle head. If you look at the Renoir, you'll see only a blob of color, which gives the *impression* of a head of a watering can, without showing the actual holes.

This one small comparison can launch you into a little discourse on the artistic style of impressionism, which began in later nineteenth-century France. I had an art teacher once describe this type of painting as "a nearsighted person's view of distant things, without his glasses on." In other words, the artist's quick impression of a scene or object or people is what is rendered.

If you look very closely at Beatrix Potter's illustration of Peter in a wheelbarrow watching Mr. McGregor hoeing (*scratch, scritch*), you'll notice the trees in the background are rendered in a rather impressionistic style, unlike her watering can. A few broad washes of color give the impression of trees and leaves closer and farther away. Here you have two distinct styles in one picture, and you can point out the precision of one versus the vagueness—the "impressionism"—of the other.

Children in a classroom may have access to watercolor paint sets, which lend themselves to impressionistic pieces. Library kids are more likely to have crayons around. It can be fun for children to look outdoors and try an impressionist painting or drawing of what they see in a quick glance.

Any reproductions of Claude Monet's water lilies, or his *Impression, Sunrise* (which gave the movement its name) could be brought in, along with works of such other impressionist artists as Degas and Pissaro. You could even get into the related style of pointillist art, where dots replace broad slashes of color to create images. If you can find a reproduction of Seurat's *Sunday Afternoon on the Grande Jatte* (1886), it will serve as an example.

You can bring the concept of pointillism right up into today by showing some of the large photographs in your local morning newspaper. Show the children that if they look closely or use a magnifying glass, they will see that these pictures are made up of tiny dots, or points, much like a Seurat painting.

Another interesting art element you can bring in from the Peter Rabbit story is Albrecht Dürer's classic study, *Young Hare*, sketched in the year 1502. This amazingly detailed master drawing shows individual hairs all over this individual hare's long ears. It shows each eyelash and whisker. There is a nice reproduction in *Dürer, His Life and Work* by Marcel Brion as well as in most such books, and I've seen it in framed versions many times. The remarkable thing about this nearly 500–year-old drawing is that you feel you can reach out and run your fingers through the fur, and feel the sharpness of the claws. Children as young as two are instantly drawn to this rabbit, and it certainly is a pleasant way to introduce a piece of art which, you can tell them, was done almost 500 years ago.

It is also a good example of realism in art and could be used to show older children the difference between realism and the impressionism discussed earlier and the expressionism I'll be talking about after the "Litte Red Hen" story next in this chapter.

One of the themes of *Peter Rabbit* that will be instantly recognizable to preschoolers is disobeying a parent. Since children this age generally cannot write (well), encourage them instead to *talk*. You can suggest such topics as "What is the *worst* thing you did when you were very little?" or "Have you ever done something naughty and been scared by what happened?" You're very likely to get some surprising responses from this one!

Well, we've taken a simple watering can out of a story about Peter Rabbit and it took us through Renoir, impressionism, pointillism, original artwork, puppets, newspapers, group discussions, and even a little Boccherini music! That represents a pretty good bunch of arts activities for any school or library group. That's good mileage from one beat-up old watering can.

✳ ✳ ✳

"The Little Red Hen and the Grain of Wheat" is one more story involving some naughty characters, and it also illustrates how we can move from one art form to another with related themes. This classic story can be found in many places, including *Chimney Corner Stories* by Veronica Hutchinson, which Lois Lenski illustrated so well. This book has just become available again after many years out of print.

In this story, the Little Red Hen finds a grain of wheat and everyone else is too lazy to help her with the steps involved to turn it into bread. The naughty—or lazy—duck and cat and dog won't help plant the wheat, cut it, take it to the mill to be ground into flour, or make it into bread.

A few simple puppets or stuffed animals (and slices of bread) can give your story a chance to rise off the page and come into the story room or classroom with you. If you use volunteer children instead for your characters, they'll have a chance to ham it up and act lazy and petulant in refusing to do any of the work.

When it comes time to eat the bread, of course, they are very willing. The Little Red Hen, however, refuses to let them, choosing instead to share it with her chicks.

To bring arts elements in after such a story with the fourto-six or seven-year-old crowd, get ahold of a big book like M. E. Tralbaut's *Vincent Van Gogh*. Van Gogh (1852–90) painted such planting-in-the-fields works as *Harvesting Wheat in the Alpilles Plain* and *In the Field*, both of which have expressionistic elements in them.

"Does the sky really look like that?" you might ask the children. You can even show them the more exaggerated expressionistic swirls of *Starry Night*, explaining that Van Gogh painted what he *felt* when he looked at a scene, not a photographic reality. I remember my own art teacher paraphrasing the artist Paul Gauguin's explanation of expressionism: "If an artist sees the tree as if it's red, he paints a red tree." If Van Gogh *felt* the sky was full of swirling energy and force, he painted it with swirls and bolts of color. An impressionist would have recreated the natural *look* of the sky instead.

This can be fun to try with the children old enough to understand the idea—at least five. Have them create an expressionistic drawing of their school or the playground or a park or a teacher—or the librarian!

It's a long way from the fields of the Little Red Hen to Van Gogh's fields, but it's an interesting way to introduce a couple of arts on a related theme.

✳ ✳ ✳

Let's update naughty creatures about a century and look at the story of a bad little girl named Splodger. The girl's name is really Kate, but when her mother asks who tracked mud into the house, or made a mess, Kate says that "Splodger did it" in *Splodger* by Paul Dowling.

Unlike Peter Rabbit, Kate is a habitual offender. She announces that Splodger never goes to bed when she's supposed to, like other children. She stands in front of her brother's TV set, so he can't see. She throws her toys and clothes all over her room, as well as the sheets and blankets. She even runs away with her Dad's sandwich and eats it herself!

When Mom erupts like a volcano and asks who made the mess in the room, Kate explains as usual that Splodger did it. Mom means business now, however, and insists that Splodger better clean it up. The girl makes a feeble attempt to disassociate herself from the bad Splodger, countering that she's really Kate. At this point, though, it appears that the name game is done for! You feel control will soon be reestablished.

Some nifty musical background for this humorous story of crashing toys and misbehavior can be found in an off-beat classical piece called "The Toy Symphony." It was composed for children's whistles and horns to mingle freely with a few traditional instruments. No one knows for sure who wrote this musical joke. It may have been Haydn, or it may have been Mozart's father, Leopold, or it may have been someone else. At any rate, it's full of mischief—just like Splodger. (I mean Kate.)

As a conversation starter or a topic for a classroom essay, you might ask the kids if they can remember the maddest a parent ever got at them, and the reason for it. Did their parent ever boil over like Splodger's exasperated mother?

Again, you can expect the unexpected to result from that question, whether you ask it of preschoolers, elementary school children, teens, adults, or even senior citizens! I used to teach a creative writing class at the night school, and I've tried the question on retirees. One elderly man still remembered the childhood misdeed of putting a cat in a pillow case, whirling it 'round and 'round, and hurling it through the air in the backyard! He also still remembers how furious his mother was when she discovered this game in progress. (The cat emerged intact.)

Splodger is a fun story to use with a puppet stage. Most of the other stories I've mentioned in this book can be enhanced by almost any informal puppet box or curtain, but *Splodger* could really use a large stage. The explosive nature of the child herself can be expressed through flying teddy bears, blankets, doll clothing, pillows, etc. from backstage. In a library story hour, these over-the-stage antics have always drawn howls of laughter from both kids and parents. The unexpected is part of the art of puppetry, and flying objects are certainly unexpected.

Rough-and-tumble children's play has also found its way into fine art. You might want to show a reproduction of Winslow Homer's schoolyard scene *Snap the Whip*, which depicts a moving, falling line of children in the schoolyard with hands joined, acting out a whip-cracking motion game. These children are getting rid of their pent-up energies in a more socially acceptable way than our girl Splodger did, but she may have fit in well with this raucous gang.

A Sample Arts-Related Story Hour
Theme: Mischief
Ages 5–7

Story: *The Tale of Peter Rabbit* (Beatrix Potter)
Music: "Minuet" (Boccherini)
Puppets & props: Four rabbits, farmer, watering can.
Art reproductions: *Girl with a Watering Can* (Renoir)
        Young Hare (Dürer)
Art concept: Impressionism
Activity: Draw or paint an impressionistic rendition of the view outside, or the room you're in, or a person in the room. (If you use the story with children 2 to 4 years old, just tell them to "take a quick look and draw what you see.")

References

Books:

Brion, Marcel. *Dürer, His Life and Work*. Tudor, 1960.
Dowling, Paul. *Splodger*. Houghton Mifflin, 1991.
"The Little Red Hen and the Grain of Wheat." In *Chimney Corner Stories* collected and retold by Veronica S. Hutchinson. Linnet Books, (1925) 1992.
Potter, Beatrix. *The Tale of Peter Rabbit*. Warne, 1903.
Tralbaut, M. E. *Vincent Van Gogh*. Viking, 1969.

Cassettes:

Boccherini, Luigi. "Minuet." *The Rage of 1710*. Vox/Turnabout. CT-4713.
Haydn, Franz Joseph (?). "The Toy Symphony." *Prokofiev's "Peter and the Wolf" and Haydn's "Toy Symphony."* Angel. 35638.

6

Silly Stories, with Popular and Jazz Music

(and a Couple of Arias)

Byron Barton's book, *Jack and Fred*, qualifies as silly enough to open this chapter.

Jack is a rabbit who befriends a sad-looking dog in the street. Jack offers the dog his ice cream cone, and tries to ask his mother if he can keep the dog. Before the words come out of his mouth, however, Mom shoos the dog away.

Jack then dresses the dog up in a pair of pants and a shirt, introducing him as a new friend. The dog eats at the dinner table with the family, and then watches television and beds down with Jack. The new "friend" strikes the parents as so funny-looking they decide it would be better for the boy to have a pet.

The next day they all go to the pet shop. The choice narrows to three: a talking bird, a monkey, or an affectionate snake. Jack tells his parents that he likes all three, but they are still not his first choice. He then unveils his surprise. He starts undressing Fred. Jack explains that Fred is the pet he really wants. Surprised that Fred is really a dog, the parents let their most clever boy keep him.

A Dixieland version of "Goofus" by Joe "Fingers" Carr from the album, *Joe "Fingers" Carr—His Happy Piano and Orchestra*, fits very well with this happy and silly story.

You might look for a related arts theme of affection for dogs to show with the story. In Renoir's famous *Luncheon of the Boating Party* (1881), the young lady feels so much affection for her dog (just as Jack did for Fred) that she has him right up on the table with her. She lifts the little pooch under his front legs and seems to be making kissing noises near his face. The faithful mutt is a little taken aback by all the attention, but seems to be enjoying it.

The picture is reproduced often, in such books as *Renoir* by Sophie Monneret, and is available in many library collections of framed reproductions.

A silly-enough activity here could be to demonstrate, yourself, an imitation of your own pet or pets, and have some of the children try it. I use Barney, our black Labrador, watching intently for our daughter to throw a ball, and then falling all over himself in his haste to retrieve it and do it again. The kids can imitate their dogs, cats, birds, gerbils, etc. in similar typical actions (with a verbal explanation of what's happening!)

✳ ✳ ✳

A recent Newbery Award winner is *Joyful Noise*, the unusual participatory poetry book Paul Fleishman has put together to be read aloud by two people. Some of the fascinating insect depictions in this book can offer delightful silliness, which can be emphasized even more by a touch of background music. For instance, two romantic "Book Lice" prove that opposites attract: one can be found in Agatha Christie books, while the other prefers Shakespeare.

In the case of this title, we should be especially careful not to let music detract. We're dealing with poetry here, and if we use any music at all, it really just has to stay in the background, adding a touch of mood. Something light and romantic is nice for our book lice couple. We couldn't use the pounding rhythms of Paula Abdul's "Opposites Attract," despite the appropriate title. Music with lyrics overwhelms a story being told, and would devastate poetry being read. Ray Conniff's light and easy version of "(If It Takes Forever) I Will Wait for You" from Ray Conniff's *World of Hits* works nicely—but keep it low. Any similar easy-listening, somewhat romantic piece would do well with *Joyful*

Noise. Children could be chosen in pairs to read aloud some of the other excellent pieces of poetry for two voices in this book.

＊＊＊

Lois Duncan provides us with a different variety of silliness in her picture book, *The Birthday Moon.* Artist Susan Davis must have thought so too, as her illustrations are moving and inspired.

This story-in-a-poem offers to give "you" a moon for your next birthday. It would be full, on a string like a balloon. Since it's round, you could use it as a coin to buy candy.

If, however, your birthday falls on a day on which there is only a half-moon, you can have a moon-like bowl, which you can fill with ice cream or cherries or soup.

If it's a quarter-moon, you could use it as a bow to shoot shimmering arrows that fireflies can follow if they're lost. Or use it as a harp. Nothing makes music as sweet as the moon.

Henry Mancini's "Moon River" is a gentle and appropriate piece for this story but again, use an instrumental version rather than one with lyrics. Quincy Jones's album, *Quincy Jones Explores the Music of Henry Mancini,* is one of many orchestral versions available. Of course, if you want to stress that spiderweb harp image, take your pick of music from the chapter here on classical harp music.

＊＊＊

Since we're talking about Henry Mancini, let's look at how we could use another of his musical compositions, "Baby Elephant Walk." The musical depiction of an elephant clomping along makes a nice background for a story like Miriam Young's *If I Rode an Elephant.*

The boy in this story vows that when he is bigger he will ride elephants. Then he imaginatively takes us on a world tour showing us how he would ride these elephants in different countries and situations.

In Siam (Thailand) he would ride an Asian elephant, the kind with small ears. The boy tells us how this elephant can uproot a tree with its trunk or delicately pluck a dandelion without breaking it.

In the jungle the boy would watch the mother elephants carrying their newborn babies in their trunks.

In India the youngster would start a babysitting service with an elephant as the world's largest babysitter. Or he would sit on top of one in a wedding procession, watching the bride atop another elephant in her throne-like *howdah* chair. Or the boy would become a *mahout*, to train a work elephant for dragging logs to the river. Or he would be a *skikari*, a guide on an elephant, leading safaris.

As the boy finally dreams of riding in his own *howdah*, dressed as a clown on top of a circus elephant, we find an opportunity to parade puppets on a stage behind the storyteller. The elephant leads a procession of ponies, tigers, gorillas, lions, monkeys, and zebras. Nothing like a puppet parade to end a story on a lively note!

✳ ✳ ✳

There's another popular tune on the Ray Conniff album which you've probably known without knowing the title. It is called "Alley Cat." It's a tune which portrays a cat leisurely roaming around in an alley, perhaps poking through garbage cans and trash, ambling along in a carefree mood. I like to use it with *Mrs. Switch*, Syd Hoff's 1966 book about the last living witch and her cat. Much of this story is about the cat.

To begin, Mrs. Switch decides that there is no point in being a lone witch, so she buys a house in suburbia with all the regular folks.

She promptly enrolls her cat in obedience school. Here we can have some fun with puppets behind the storyteller: the cat learns not to attack helpless birds anymore; then he learns that it is not acceptable, in proper society, to sit on a fence and meow; it is also not proper to bring people bad luck. (A puppet can trip and fall here.)

The cat observes such excellent behavior that it becomes the mascot of the community bowling team. Mrs. Switch and her cat soon become favorites around the neighborhood, and the families give a dinner in their honor.

Mrs. Switch, unfortunately, makes a tactical error. She begins to tell the children stories about ghosts and goblins and witches on broomsticks. The children don't believe that anyone could fly on a broomstick, so Mrs. Switch and her cat *show* them. The sight of the former witch and her well-behaved cat in the air causes great shock and anger among the neighbors. Mrs. Switch and her cat quickly become social outcasts.

The long cold winter finally sets in and brings a tremendous amount of snow. A child is ill, and the doctor can't come because he is stuck in the snow. The seemingly impossible-to-solve crisis is solved by Mrs. Switch and her faithful cat, who hop onto their broomstick and pick up the doctor. After that, of course, they become the most popular pair in town.

"Alley Cat" is perfect background for this story. The illustrations are so big and clear, you may elect not to add many puppets behind you.

As silly a story as *Mrs. Switch* may be, there's also a strong bond of affection between the lady and her cat. After all, the cat was faithful when all others deserted her. A related art work you could show—although this one has no silliness whatsoever—is Andrew Wyeth's painting, *Miss Olson* (1952). This remarkable portrait of the crippled Christina (from his painting *Christina's World*) shows a woman cradling a kitten to herself, both with eyes closed. Wyeth admired the inner strength of the crippled woman and knew how much kittens and cats meant to her. It would not hurt to break up the silly stories theme of this chapter with a few moments of reflection on how important that kitten must have been to Miss Olson.

✳ ✳ ✳

How about trying Boots Randolph's saxophone jazz version of the comical song, "Charlie Brown" with James Marshall's version of *The Three Little Pigs*? The peppy and humorous saxophone music, about that character for whom nothing seems to go right, fits the hapless wolf—who ends up in the cook pot.

Silly Stories with Popular and Jazz Music

The first two little pigs wind up as dinner for the wolf because they foolishly build their houses out of straw and sticks. The more practical third builds his out of bricks, and the wolf has to resort to trickery to get near him.

First, the wolf invites him to pick parsnips. The pig arrives an hour early, and is safely home before the wolf comes to eat him. The pig also comes early to meet the wolf for apple-picking, and manages to escape harm, by throwing an apple at the wolf and hightailing it back home. A third escape is more than the wolf can stand.

The wolf yells that it's his dinnertime and jumps down the chimney of the little brick house. The pig agrees about dinner, but disagrees as to who will be the main course. He pushes a big iron pot onto the fire and catches the falling wolf, who makes a substantial supper.

✳ ✳ ✳

Now let's return to the music of Henry Mancini for a piece called "Bird Brain," also on the Quincy Jones album. You can tell from the title that this is an appropriate tune to use with Chris Riddell's picture story, *Bird's New Shoes*. The story concerns "keeping up with the Joneses," fashion-wise. The characters caught up in this activity are all animals.

Bird shows up one day wearing a nice new pair of shoes. He tells the admiring rat that the shoes are indeed the latest thing. The rat simply must have a pair, too, and makes a fashion statement of his own by adding a bow tie to his new pair of shoes. He shows the warthog, who also feels compelled to rush out and obtain the latest in trendy clothing. The warthog adds yet another accessory to the look—a hat.

This pattern goes on through a buffalo, a rabbit, a goat, and a snake. Each adds an article of apparel such as a vest, shorts, sunglasses, and jeans. At the end, Bird removes his shoes—in order to be different.

Children and adults can understand the essential silliness of the animals scurrying to duplicate the fashion statements of others and their comical attempts at one-upsmanship. These things are recognizable as all-too-familiar human behaviors as well. "Bird Brain" is a musical piece which not only describes the activities of the story musically—but verbally as well!

✳ ✳ ✳

For Anna Standon's *The Singing Rhinoceros*, I'd like to offer a different approach to finding a musical match-up. I will break my rule of not using music with lyrics with a story. Not only that, I will use Placido Domingo singing grand opera! It does happen to fit into this story perfectly—as an integral part, no less, not just as background music.

The rhinoceros is very popular at his home in the zoo, as he is extremely good-natured and always happy. He is also kind, gentle, polite, and beloved by everyone.

I like to use a poster board cut-out of a rhino as the puppet for this fellow. In fact, since it is a large animal, I use two poster boards taped together.

One day, the rhinoceros gets loose from his cage and sets out to explore the town. He cannot understand why the teachers slam the school door in his face. He is puzzled that a man climbs up a tree and says "Shoo." Nevertheless, he has a grand time listening to all the birds singing.

The rhinoceros then wanders into the garden of the local music director. What bliss! He begins to feast on the sumptuous flowers, and then sits down in the middle of the idyllic garden, listening to the bees buzzing. He is so happy that he begins to sing. The music director can not believe the magnificent voice he is hearing!

This is the point where I bring in Placido Domingo. I have a tape called *The Magic of Placido Domingo*, which offers us selections from *La Bohème*, *Martha*, *Pagliacci*, *Rigoletto* and more operas. I've used "La donna è mobile" from Verdi's *Rigoletto*, but any of the others would do just as well. Any male opera solo would serve the purpose.

The music director arranges for the singing rhinoceros to live in the garden and to appear at the local music festival. The king himself comes to hear the famous singing rhinoceros perform: spotlights concentrate their beams on him, and once again, the magnificent sounds of Domingo fill the story room. To top it all off, a real princess gives the singing rhino a bouquet of flowers.

The combination of grand opera being used with a silly story like this helps intensify the humor for young children.

＊ ＊ ＊

This is one of the rare opportunities in which opera would actually fit right into the story. The other that comes to mind is Gene Zion's *Harry and the Lady Next Door*, in which Harry the dog cannot *stand* the operatic warblings of the next door neighbor. You could use some arias by Maria Callas or Joan Sutherland or Licia Albanese—or any other female opera singer available— for this story. The more serious the music, the more silly it makes the story, which is exactly the effect we want! And, there is plenty of opportunity for puppet involvement, as you will see.

Harry's owners invite the lady to their house and, sure enough, she sings. Rather than biting her leg, Harry bites the piano leg. He is sent outside and the wind carries the lady's sheet music out the door, to Harry's delight.

Harry finds a herd of cows, and he loves their beautiful mooing sounds—so he leads the herd to the lady's house, to show her what good singing really is. Undaunted, the lady warbles on, and Harry is banished to the dog house.

Eventually Harry finds a firemen's oompah band, grabs the leader's baton, and makes the musicians chase him to the lady's house. The band plays on, but the lady continues to sing. Again Harry is banished to the dog house.

At the town singing contest, Harry finds a watering can with two frogs inside and puts it behind the lady as she sings. When the frogs jump up on her head and shoulders, she hits such unique high notes that she wins the contest.

Her prize is a boat trip abroad, and the departing ship's foghorns are the sweetest music Harry has ever heard!

One cute activity you can try after such tales is to have the children do some *verbal* imitations this time. Ask them all to try to sound like Harry's cows mooing together, then Harry's frog. They could also try to sing together like the lady next door, with her high voice, and the big singing rhino with his deeper voice. They could finally howl like Harry did at the neighbor.

Another interesting related arts activity is to search for dogs in famous works of art. For example, in *Paintings by the Masters* there's a reproduction of *The Children of Charles I* by Anthony van Dyck (painted between 1632 and 1641 when van Dyck was official court painter to Charles I). In their silks and satins and lace, Charles's boy and two girls also had their beloved two pet dogs by their sides while they posed for their royal portraits. It is interesting to point out that kids 400 years ago had something in common with kids today. It's a good way to bring art into any dog story.

Going a couple of centuries beyond van Dyck, you could also show Renoir's *Portrait of Madame Charpentier and Her Children* from 1878. Not only do the kids have their huge and faithful dog along for the portrait, but one of the two girls is sitting right on top of him. The dog lies there peacefully, despite the girl's weight and the apparent jabbing of both her shoes. This is the epitome of the faithful dog!

✳ ✳ ✳

Mucky Moose by Jonathan Allen is one genuinely funny silly story! I stumbled across a thoroughly lovable brown and tan, three-foot-high stuffed moose in a Goodwill store about a year ago, and grabbed it specifically to become "Mucky." It is one of my largest puppet characters at the moment.

Besides finding a place to store the giant moose, the story presents several other absolutely unique challenges to the art of seat-of-the-pants puppeteering: how to simulate a gas mask on a wolf puppet, how to attach a clothespin to the wolf's nose, and how to simulate a blind man being led by the wolf!

First let's look at the story. I start out by asking the kids, " 'Mucky'—what does that name sound like to you?" They often reply, "Yucky," which is pretty accurate. I explain that our moose is called Mucky because he lives in the swamp with his friends the frogs, flies, birds, and skunks. He is so yucky and smelly and dirty that the skunks applaud when he comes near them.

Now let's stop right here for a moment and consider backing up the story with puppets. After much shopping around, I found a three-inch rubber fly in a novelty store. To make it move, I impaled it on a spare card catalog rod—which gives my puppeteers the ability to buzz the fly around the moose. I may be stretching the definition of "art form" here, but children's librarians will understand!

The R. Dakin Company makes some terrific skunk puppets, which I bought. However, you can also draw these animals on poster board, or cut them out of a nature magazine or book and mount them on rods. The birds I use are either hand puppets, stuffed or styrofoam versions from Christmas arrangements, Easter baskets, etc., on rods.

Let's move along. There is a wolf in the story (R. Dakin also makes a great wolf puppet) who wants a moose for dinner, and since Mucky is the largest, the wolf approaches our hero. One good whiff of the moose, however, renders this wily predator unconscious. (In the book, the wolf turns green, but there is a limit to how technologically advanced our puppetry can be.)

The wolf eventually returns with a clothespin on his nose, announcing in a stuffy voice that he is now going to eat the offending moose for dinner. Your puppeteers will have to rehearse finding a part of the wolf's nose which can hold the clothespin securely, without its falling off in the middle of your story. The appearance of the puppet with a clothespin on its nose is, however, a sure-fire laugh producer. You or your puppeteer can pinch your nostrils shut and demonstrate the sound of the wolf talking through a clothespin.

Mucky finds the nasal threats difficult to decipher and tells the wolf to remove the clothespin and repeat the message. When the wolf obliges, he is immediately overcome with another whiff of powerful odor. After a week in bed, the wolf returns, this time with a gas mask over his muzzle. This may sound like a complicated puppetry problem—finding a miniature gas mask—but, really, a paper cup over the wolf's nose works very well and is another guaranteed laugh-getter.

Locating his intended prey, the wolf again announces his plan to eat Mucky for dinner. The scientifically astute moose then points out that the wolf can't possibly chew on anything unless he removes the gas mask. Seeing the logic of this, the wolf pulls off the mask, turns purple, and falls unconscious once again. For our finale, our puppeteers need a male doll, and a pair of sunglasses to transform him into a blind man. Run a piece of string from the blind man's hand to the wolf's neck, and presto! our reformed villain has become a seeing-eye wolf.

Mucky goes back to the smelliest part of the swamp and lives happily ever after with his friends the frogs, the skunks, and the birds.

As you can tell, this story is a feast for the puppeteer. As far as music goes, I like to pick an instrument that sounds a bit silly to begin with to go with the story. A bassoon or an oboe or a piccolo come to mind. The bassoon seems to conjure up more of a feeling of a deep, murky swamp. Mozart and Vivaldi are among those who wrote concerti for the bassoon. The closing movement of Mozart's "Bassoon Concerto in B flat Major" works well with the mood of the story.

A Sample Arts-Related Story Hour Program
Theme: Dogs and Cats—Silly Stories
Ages preschool and early elementary

1. *Participation song*: "Bingo"
2. *Musical story*
   Story: *Harry and the Lady Next Door* (Gene Zion)
   Music: Licia Albanese (or any female opera star) singing your choice of arias—Puccini's, for example.
   Musical mood: High culture, contrasting with the silliness of the annoying lady neighbor's singing in the story. The contrast creates more humor.
   Puppet participation: You'll need a dog, a woman, and various onlookers.
   Art works: *The Children of Charles I* (van Dyck); *Madame Charpentier and Her Children* (Renoir)
   Activity: Let children imitate Harry's cows, frogs, neighbor-lady, and howling.
3. *Musical story*
   Story: *Mrs. Switch* (Syd Hoff)
   Music: "Alley Cat"
   Musical mood: Comical, suggesting a cat on the prowl.
   Puppet participation: You'll need a witch, a cat, some neighbors and children, a broomstick, and a doctor.
   Art to show: *Miss Olson* (Wyeth)
   Coloring: You can draw and xerox a simple cat or dog for all to color with crayons.
4. *Writing or making up a story*: You can have the children write a Halloween story (or tell a made-up one) which involves a real witch and her cats, and her young witches (children) too.

References

Books:
Allen, Jonathan. *Mucky Moose*. Macmillan, 1990
Barton, Byron. *Jack and Fred*. Macmillan, 1974.

Corn, Wanda. *The Art of Andrew Wyeth.* N. Y. Graphic Society, 1973.

Duncan, Lois. *The Birthday Moon.* Viking-Kestrel, 1989.

Fleishman, Paul. *Joyful Noise: Poems for Two Voices.* Harper and Row, 1988.

Harold, Margaret, comp. *Paintings by the Masters.* Allied Publications, 1966.

Hoff, Syd. *Mrs. Switch.* G.P. Putnam's Sons, 1966.

Marshall, James. *The Three Little Pigs.* Dial, 1989.

Monneret, Sophie. *Renoir.* Henry Holt, 1989.

Riddell, Chris. *Bird's New Shoes.* Henry Holt, 1987.

Standon, Anna. *The Singing Rhinoceros.* Coward-McCann, 1963.

Young, Miriam. *If I Rode an Elephant.* Lothrop, Lee and Shepard, 1974.

Zion, Gene. *Harry and the Lady Next Door.* Harper, 1960.

Record Albums:

Albanese, Licia. *Albanese Sings Puccini.* RCA Victor, LM-2033.

"Alley Cat." *Ray Conniff's World of Hits.* Columbia. CS-9300.

"Baby Elephant Walk." *Quincy Jones Explores the Music of Henry Mancini.* Mercury. SR-60863.

"Bird Brain." *Ibid.*

"Charlie Brown." *Boots Randolph's Yakety Sax.* Monument. SLP 18002.

"Goofus." *Joe "Fingers" Carr—His Happy Piano and Orchestra.* Sears. SPS-438.

"(If It Takes Forever) I Will Wait for You." *Ray Conniff's World of Hits.* Columbia. CS-9300.

"Moon River." *Quincy Jones Explores the Music of Henry Mancini.* Mercury. SR-60863.

Mozart. Bassoon Concerto. *Mozart. Music for Winds and Brass.* Murray Hill. S-4364.

Cassette:

"La donna è mobile" from *Rigoletto* by Verdi. *The Magic of Placido Domingo.* RCA CAM 1209.

7

Puppets and the Art of Surprise

The element of surprise may well be one of the biggest delights that puppets can add to a story program. In this chapter, we'll surprise our children with puppets and props which do not stay where they belong. We will see jewelry, flowers, frogs, snakes, a horse, a prince, cups of water, chalk dust, and baby powder all fly from the puppet stage, often right into the audience!

A note of caution, however. The storyteller should first ascertain if there are children present who suffer from asthma or other bronchial problems. If so, make sure those children are far from the scene of action—or better yet, perhaps pass up the opportunity to use some of these "special effects."

Now let's look at a story called "The Fairies" in Shari Lewis's *One Minute Fairy Tales*. In this version of a French story, we meet a nasty woman with two daughters. One is just as nasty and rotten as mom, but the other takes after her father—kind and good. The nasty woman favors the nasty daughter, and makes the nice one do all the work. When the mother sends her sweet daughter to the well to fetch water, the young woman meets a fairy disguised as a thirsty old woman. The fairy asks for a drink, and the girl graciously complies.

To the girl's surprise, the fairy gives her a gift. Every time she begins to speak, jewels and flowers come pouring out of her mouth.

You may be able to put together a box of plastic jewelry similar to what a staff member brought me back from the Mardi Gras in New Orleans. You may also be able to build up a collection of dime store plastic flowers. Here is your chance to use them with the characters. Try to imagine the surprise of your child listeners when the girl tries to explain her meeting with the fairy to her nasty mother—and necklaces and flowers are catapulted from backstage each time she speaks! My puppeteers let them go right over the stage and onto the floor. (You may want to have a helper on guard in front of the stage to prevent a scramble if the children go for the jewels!)

As usual, I am up front telling the story, while my helpers are behind the stage working the puppets and props. I always have plenty of kids volunteering to be puppeteers, especially when they learn that they don't have to say anything—or memorize lines.

Meanwhile, the nasty old woman decides to send her beloved nasty daughter to the well, hoping for the same golden results. This is called "going to the well once too often." The girl meets the same fairy in disguise, and is asked for a drink. Nasty as ever, the girl complies but badgers the old woman to hurry up.

This time, the fairy's gift is equally appropriate: every time the crabby girl speaks, out of her mouth come frogs and snakes! You can imagine how surprised the kids are when these creatures start to fly off the puppet stage! I have quite a few stuffed frogs (including bean-bags). I also have a three-foot stuffed snake from Miami's MetroZoo, and the grand finale—a comical ten-foot stuffed snake. That represents the ultimate in the element of airborne surprise! Children won't forget this story.

As a moral to the story the good fairy puppet returns, revealing herself and explaining her lesson to all: In this life, you get what you give. In this case, we've given a memorable, fun-filled, story program with the puppets providing all kinds of laughs through the element of surprise. Kids love a show like this!

✳ ✳ ✳

Next let's flip through the same Shari Lewis book and find her version of the Persian tale, "The Flying Horse." In this story, we find a ninety-year-old magician who owns a magical wooden horse. If you twist one pin, it flies. If you twist the other, it returns. (Puppeteers: wrapping a heavy coat hanger wire around a stuffed animal version of the horse can propel our star skyward when the time comes.)

Well, the ninety-year-old magician decides that it's time to get married. He goes to the king and offers to trade the magical horse for the king's daughter. The king likes that magical horse awfully much, so he agrees.

The girl laments about the situation to her brother, imploring him to get their royal father to reconsider. The magician therefore schemes to get rid of the meddlesome brother. The old magician, however, is not very good at thinking things through (which is a valuable trait for folks to develop). He cunningly shows the young man the horse, which he describes as a gift for the king. The brother asks to try it out, and the magician only tells him about the first pin. The young man twists the first pin and flies off, never to be seen again. He has no idea how to make the horse return. (Puppeteers: you need a little twine or yarn to tie the poor fellow onto the horse.) You can imagine the surprise and delight in the young audience to see these puppets fly above the stage.

Well, the old magician is happy now, for he is free to trade the magical flying horse for the lovely young daughter. Except for one problem: there's no more horse to trade! And therein lies the lesson about how important it is to think things through. Now he had no bribe, no horse, and no youth.

But *we've* had a terrific story made even livelier by puppets who surprised their young audience by not staying where they were expected to be — *on* the stage. This adds a whole bunch of giggles and gasps to this particular story.

The flying horse has a counterpart in art, and that is *The Green Horse* from Marc Chagall's world of dreams and imagination. This is certainly "a horse of a different color!" The 1956 painting can be found in Roy McMillen's *The World of Marc Chagall*. Franz Marc, another artist, did an equally colorful picture, *The Blue Horse*, which can be found in many modern art books.

An art project could encourage some young imaginations to

soar. The children could draw themselves on a flying horse. They could also write a story about where they would go on their imaginary steeds.

✳ ✳ ✳

Since we've used the Shari Lewis book twice already, how about one more time? This is another tale called "One Particular Small, Smart Boy."

In this story, a tiny little boy meets up with a giant. For these two I use a two-inch-high plastic boy and a rather large boy doll. For the special effects to come we need two paper cups full of water, a couple of rocks from outside, a plastic egg, and an open bottle of baby powder.

The small boy meets up with the giant who threatens to have the tiny tot for lunch. The boy may be small, but he is quick-thinking. He tells the giant that will not be possible, for even though he is much smaller, he is also much stronger.

The giant laughs at this, but the boy challenges him to a contest of strength to prove it. The boy has an egg and some salt in his pocket, and makes the most out of them.

First he gives the giant a rock and tells him to squeeze the water out of it. Of course, the giant can't do it, so the boy offers to show him how. The boy takes his egg, pretends he is squeezing a rock and—whoosh!—the liquid goes flying. This is when your puppeteers can fling a paper cup of water high over the stage, to the surprise and delight of the laughing audience.

I like to milk the story a little and have the giant say, "Wait a minute. Let's see you do that again!" That's why I recommend having *two* cups of water on hand.

The giant is rapidly becoming convinced. The boy, however, presses on. He boasts that he will crush a rock into salt. Taking some salt from his pocket, the tiny boy makes good on his boast. At this point, a puppeteer can squeeze a plastic bottle of baby powder and, at the same time, thrust the container upward— creating a stream of "salt" flying through the air. Again, if it gets the laugh it usually gets, have the giant say, "Wait a minute. Let's see you do that again."

Now the giant is totally convinced. The boy announces that he will now take the giant's hand and squeeze it into *mud*. The giant says, "Oh no, you won't" and runs away, never to bother that particular small, smart boy ever again.

A counterpart in the art world to the giant in the story can be found in Goya's *Colossus*, which shows a figure resembling the "Incredible Hulk" stomping through the country menacingly. This monster can be found in Alphonso Sanchez's book, *Goya*.

Since children have such a fascination with giants and monsters, you could have them draw one of their own. You could even have a contest to see who could come up with the ugliest, scariest-looking creature. Goya's *Colossus* could serve as an example of what they could create out of their own imaginations.

As I write this chapter, which used all three stories from one Shari Lewis collection, I'm happy to report that Miss Lewis has made a television comeback. Her motto is "Don't just view it, do it." Her "anti-couch potato" philosophy is based on her feeling that children go into a stoned stupor watching most television programs. Certainly anything we can do involving stories, books, puppets, art, music, drawing and writing would be our blow to strike against this passivity, and in favor of children participating in creative activities.

✳ ✳ ✳

Classrooms have something which public libraries don't always have—blackboard erasers caked with chalk dust. Let's take a look at how you can use these chalk-laden erasers with a couple of puppets to tell a Br'er Rabbit story (or any others).

"How Mr. Rabbit Succeeded in Raising a Dust" tells of the age-old dilemma faced by Molly Cottontail and all the girls: the boys won't leave them alone. The ladies in this story, however, come up with an almost-ingenious solution. It would've qualified as ingenious, except that it doesn't work.

The girls invent a contest which will get rid of the pesty boys once and for all. If any one of the boys can knock the dust out of a big flint rock, he can have his pick of the ladies. Otherwise, they all have to go away.

One by one the gents pick up "de sludge hammer" and pound it down futilely on the rock. Nothing happens.

Br'er Rabbit, crafty as ever, sneaks around to Br'er Coon's fireplace, picks up a pair of slippers, and fills them with ashes. Then he returns to try his strength on the rock. Br'er Rabbit swings the sledge hammer over his head, jumps high in the air, clicks his ash-filled slippers together, and slams the hammer down on the rock!

Just at this point in the story, your eraser-wielding backstage volunteer claps the erasers together. Clouds of chalk dust fly skyward as Br'er Rabbit "sludges" that rock, over and over. The result is a hilarious special effect and a memorable storytelling experience. (Jerking a container of baby powder works well, too.)

Another example of this effect that pops into my mind, which I can't resist mentioning, involves Jane Thayer's *The Popcorn Dragon*. The sudden puffs of smoke from erasers or baby powder make a great visual effect for the story of this fire-breathing dragon who regains his popularity by turning his smoky flame on ears of corn, making popcorn for all the animals who previously scorned him. You could add a verse or two of "Puff the Magic Dragon" by Peter, Paul, and Mary for a chaser, also!

But back to Br'er Rabbit. This cunning critter has his pick of the gals and marries Molly Cottontail. "Here Comes the Bride" (from Wagner's *Lohengrin*) or "The Wedding March" make a nifty conclusion to this story. (You will find information about this music in chapter 2.)

✳ ✳ ✳

A note about puppet stages: I don't know how many kinds of makeshift stages I've used with storytelling in libraries, schools, churches, and so on, but I do know a stage can be simulated anywhere. A decorated cardboard box with one side cut out works well, as long as you can hide the puppets before they pop up. If you are in a position to buy a puppet stage, there is a nice lightweight one, the "WatchMe Blossom Puppet Theatre." I like it because it has a curtain which can be raised, two attachable lights, and it can be pushed by one person to wherever you want to use it or store it. I have however, previously used a room divider on wheels covered with black felt.

The point is the same as with the puppets and the "special effects": whatever you can rig up, borrow, find at garage sales, or commandeer from the broom closet might work. As for puppets, even brown lunch bags can make good hand puppets. Use buttons for eyes, cut out scraps of colored paper for noses, mouths, and ears, and paste them on. Kids have been doing this on their own forever, it seems, and then entertaining family, friends, neighbors, and even reluctant siblings—sometimes at a price!

Puppets and stages are magical things in bringing stories off the page and into the room. These puppets and stages can be put together with next to nothing. Lack of a budget can't stop a real puppeteer! All you need is a little imagination and enthusiasm, and you can go a long, long way!

A Sample Arts-Related Story Hour Program
Theme: Surprises
Ages 5–8

Story: "The Fairies" (Shari Lewis)
Puppets: Two daughters, mother, old woman, fairy, frogs, snakes
Props: Plastic jewelry, artificial flowers, cups of water

Story: "The Flying Horse" (Shari Lewis)
Puppets: Magician, king, princess, prince, horse
Art: *The Green Horse* (Marc Chagall)
    The Blue Horse (Franz Marc)
Art project: Draw yourself on a flying horse
Writing: Using the drawings as illustrations, have the children write or tell a story about where they would go on their imaginary flying horses.

Story: "One Particular Small, Smart Boy" (Shari Lewis)
Puppets: Boy, giant
Props: Plastic egg, two rocks, bottle of baby powder, two paper cups full of water
Art: *The Colossus* (Goya)
Art project: Draw a giant-monster

Story: "How Mr. Rabbit Succeeded in Raising a Dust" (Harris)
Puppets: Two or more rabbits, a raccoon, miscellaneous animals
Props: Hammer, rock, chalky erasers
Music: "Here Comes the Bride" (the wedding march from Wagner's *Lohengrin*)
Musical mood: Wedding ceremony
Activity: Pantomime time! Ask each child to "sludge" a rock, first with no result, and then with dust flying. A little demonstration may help here: pick up the heavy hammer (*groan*); raise it over your head (*pant, pant*); then bring it down with full force (*aahh—grunt!*) A clap of erasers from your volunteer could signal when the rock was truly "sludged."

References

Books:

Harris, Joel Chandler. *Uncle Remus: His Songs and Sayings.* Grosset and Dunlap, 1921.
Lewis, Shari. *One Minute Fairy Tales.* Doubleday, 1985.
McMillen, Roy. *The World of Marc Chagall.* Doubleday, 1968.
Sanchez, Alphonso. *Goya.* Henry Holt, 1989.
Thayer, Jane. *The Popcorn Dragon.* Morrow Junior Books, 1953.

Record Albums:

Wagner, Richard. "Wedding March" ("Here Comes the Bride") from *Lohengrin. The Hollywood Bowl Wedding Album.* Hollywood Bowl Symphony Orchestra and Roger Wagner Chorale. Capitol SP 8653.

Compact Disc:

"Puff the Magic Dragon." *Moving.* Peter, Paul, and Mary. W.B.R. 1473–2.

8

Puppet Masks—
Children as Puppets

All through this book I've been advocating adding puppets or
stuffed animals to the telling and reading of stories. There are
certain stories, however, which are nearly impossible to match
with puppets or stuffed animals, but call for cut-out masks instead. In the following stories, for example, it's pretty difficult to
come up with eleven puppets or stuffed tigers all at once, or eight
Chinese puppets of various ages, or a tooth fairy.

* * *

Let's take a story from Haiti, *The Banza: A Haitian Story*,
retold by Diane Wolkstein. This book explains that in Haiti, the
storyteller often will say, "Cric," meaning, "Do you want to hear
a story?" The children will reply, "Crac," meaning, "Yes!" (Inci-
dentally, this led the Miami-Dade Public Library to name their
televised storytelling series "Cric Crac." North Miami, as well as
Miami and all of Dade County, Florida, have large and growing
Haitian populations).

At any rate, *The Banza* (a banjo) is the story of the friendship
between Cabree the goat and Teegra the young tiger. Although
these two are supposed to be natural enemies, they develop a
friendship. Being forced to share the same cave during a thunderstorm has a way of bringing folks closer together. Cabree and
Teegra have a great time.

After the storm, Teegra goes home but returns to give
Cabree a present—the *banza*, or banjo. Teegra advises the goat

always to keep the banza over her heart, for someday her heart and the banjo will become one.

At this point in the story, you could show the children what a banjo sounds like by playing a bit of banjo music from a recording such as *Feuding Banjos*.

As for puppets, what comes next in the story is beyond my collection. I happen to own one goat and one tiger puppet, which I use for my main characters, but now Cabree is in the woods and runs into ten tigers, which are, you recall, her natural enemies.

This took a little doing in my puppet manufacturing department. I used ten pieces of yellow poster board and drew the general outlines of ten tigers from the book. (The one with the fancy hat took longest!) I outlined the teeth and individual black stripes on each tiger, cut out the shapes—and then I got smart. I formed a club of after-school latchkey kids and asked them to color in the stripes with black magic markers and to dab white-out on each tooth. They loved doing it, and pretty soon I had my cast of characters. (Another good idea is to make friends with your local dry cleaner. Mine gives me wire clothes hangers, which I attach with masking tape to the back of each mask, leaving a handle to hold at the bottom).

So now I had ten tiger puppets-on-sticks, and with the appearance of the tigers in the story, I passed them out to children (chosen previously) to enact what follows with our goat, Cabree. (A staff member "directs" the tigers while I read the story). With the arrival of the tigers, at first Cabree panics. But then she picks up the banza and starts ad-libbing a very brave-sounding song while she strums—something about how she ate ten fat tigers raw the day before.

Upon hearing this concert, five tigers leave to fetch Madame Cabree a drink of water. They never return. Cabree repeats the song to the remaining five fat tigers, then to three, then finally to the one in the hat—who begs for mercy.

Cabree lets the last tiger leave, on the condition that he deliver a message to Teegra: that today the goat's heart and the banza have become one.

This method of storytelling with a bit of theatrical art is fun for the kids. They can be in the show, but they don't have to say anything, and they get applause from the audience at the end — a great confidence-builder!

After the performance it is appropriate to show a beautiful book of Haitian paintings, *Where Art Is Joy* by Selden Rodman. The vibrant, bright, colorful art of the Haitian people tells plenty about their culture and country and climate, their work and their homes, their humor and lives.

* * *

Another story where masks work well (since finding eight Chinese puppets is a bit much to hope for), is Claire Bishop's *The Five Chinese Brothers*. For this one we need the five look-alike siblings, their mother, a judge, and a little boy.

The masks can be made out of yellow poster boards, drawn on with black magic markers and held up by eight coat hangers. Again, I generally select kids from the audience who perform on their own with a little directorial help from an adult volunteer who knows the story.

The first Chinese brother can swallow the sea; the second has an iron neck. The third can stretch and stretch his legs. The fourth cannot be burned. The fifth can hold his breath indefinitely.

The little-boy part goes to someone who enjoys being a ham. At the beginning of the story he gets to run around gathering things from the floor of the sea while the first Chinese brother holds the sea water inside himself. The little boy also gets to fall over and drown when he refuses to leave the sea floor and the first Chinese brother must spit the water back.

For this (inadvertent) crime, the judge decides that the first brother must have his head chopped off. The judge allows him to go home to say goodbye to his mother, and while there, he changes places with the second brother. The second biggest ham can have the second brother's part. He gets to bend over and astonish the crowd as the executioner fails to dent his iron neck. (A good prop here is a plastic sword in a sheath. With the storyteller playing the part of executioner, there's no chance of anyone getting hurt by a zealous or "method" actor.)

When this fails, the judge decides that the accused should be drowned. The prisoner asks permission to go home and say goodbye to his old mother. While there, he changes places with the third brother who can stretch his legs. When this brother is thrown out of a boat to be drowned, he stretches his legs until he is standing securely on the bottom. (The child with this mask can make "leg-stretching" sounds of an imaginative nature. This can be very comical.)

The judge now orders that the culprit be burned. Another switch is made to the fourth brother. At this point, bring in some cut-out, collage-like poster board "flames" in red, yellow, and orange, glued together. Place these at the feet of the Chinese brother who is now tied at the stake. His comment is that it's deliciously nice and warm. You might ask your actor how he likes it and he will most likely ad lib something comical and make the rest of the kids laugh.

The exasperated judge decides to have this indestructible prisoner smothered with whipped cream and stuffed into an oven. One more trip home and our hero changes places with the sibling who can hold his breath indefinitely. Of course, this one wakes up refreshed from his nap in the oven the next morning. Ask your actor to stretch and tell how good he feels.

This story was originally written in 1938 before violence became much of a conscious issue in children's books. I tried it with a very sweet fourth grade teacher a few years ago, wondering if it was a bad choice because of all the violence. Gentle Mrs. Friedman and her class liked it so much that she has requested this story every year when she walks to the library with her fourth graders! I guess it's such a plain good old yarn that its redeeming qualities make up for the questionable ones. In this respect, it is much like classic folk and fairy tales from the Grimms or Andersen.

The end of the story gives a chance to introduce some Chinese painting as a tie-in. Landscapes in particular will appeal for their distinctive mountains, flowers, trees, etc. There are many books and reproductions available, and it's not necessary to single out a particular artist.

✳ ✳ ✳

One other story which lends itself to puppet masks perhaps more than puppets is *The Real Tooth Fairy* by Marilyn Kaye. Although I've gathered hundreds of puppets and stuffed animals over the years, I've yet to come up with an appropriate tooth fairy! It's easier to make a poster board cut-out mask, like the beautiful one in Marilyn Kaye's book. Some ethereal music such as the opening of the "Moonlight Sonata" (Beethoven) could accompany the regal one's appearance.

The younger kids show interest in this story because they know that *something* has been to their house too. . . .

Several other characters present themselves as candidates for masks for our actors: one female teacher; our heroine Elise; her mother; her best friend Susan; her classmate Ben; and Ben's father. Your own family (or your staff's) may provide you with a real tooth—or you may opt for a chicklet—or a cut-out poster-board version.

In the book, Elise stays awake, determined to get a glimpse of the real tooth fairy, who is due to collect a fallen tooth and leave a reward, as her friend Susan explains. To her great astonishment, Elise learns that her own mother is the tooth fairy! What could beat that?

Elise tells some kids the secret. Ben later has to tell Elise that she's wrong: Ben's *father* is the tooth fairy!

The mother gracefully explains to Elise that the real tooth fairy is trying to be careful not to scare any children, so she works through the parents. At the end of the book, however -yes!—the truly real, winged tooth fairy does reveal herself in all her ethereal splendor.

✳ ✳ ✳

Using puppet masks is mini-creative dramatics, and it involves the children very directly in the progress of the story. It demands improvisation in the form of grunts, squeaks, and other inventive noises; motion; and even dialogue. It can be as interactive as you want it to be. This form of puppetry works particularly well with an active group of kids. Your only real problem is making sure all of them can be given the chance to help "act it out."

While the extra effort on your part may take more time than you would wish, the results will more than repay it. And besides, you will have added to your stock of puppets with a whole new cast of characters for other shows as well.

There are of course people who can make elaborate masks out of papier mâché or any number of materials. This book, however, concerns itself with quick, simple things that can be produced week after week all year long. Most libraries seem to have at least one person on the staff or among the volunteers who can take a magic marker (black), copy a reasonably accurate depiction of a few characters in a book, color them in with other magic markers and tape a rod to the back with enough of a handle for a child to hold onto.

This represents the full extent of my ability with crafts, but thankfully you can build an entire full-fledged theater repertoire with nothing more than one minimal artist, a box of magic markers, some poster boards and a pair of scissors. In public libraries, making magic out of little is often a way of life!

A Sample Arts-Related Story Hour Program
Featuring Puppet Masks
Theme: Escaping Danger
Ages 4–9

1. Story: *The Banza: A Haitian Story* (Diane Wolkstein)
   Puppet masks: Ten cut-out poster board tigers for ten children
   Puppets: Goat, small tiger
   Music: Banjo music
   Art book: *Where Art Is Joy* (Selden Rodman)
2. Story: *The Five Chinese Brothers* (Claire Bishop)
   Puppet masks: Five brothers, a little boy, a judge, the mother
   Props: Executioner's sword, poster board flames for a fire
   Art: Chinese landscape paintings

References

Books:

Bishop, Claire H. *The Five Chinese Brothers*. Sandcastle Books, 1989.
Kaye, Marilyn. *The Real Tooth Fairy*. Harcourt Brace Jovanovich, 1990.
Rodman, Selden. *Where Art Is Joy*. Ruggels de Latour, 1988.
Wolkstein, Diane. *The Banza: A Haitian Story*. Dial, 1981.

Compact Disc:

Weissberg, Eric, et al. *Feuding Banjos*. Delux 1040.

9
Dog Stories

Syd Hoff's 1964 book, *Lengthy*, is still one of his all-time funniest. This one is kind of a "horizontal tall tale," a humorous story about a dachshund who looks about twenty-five feet long.

Having established that tall tale premise, Hoff follows it logically through a variety of situations. What other dog, Hoff asks, could a long line of children all pet at the same time? What other dog could they use as a jump rope?

A poor old lady tries her best to take care of Lengthy. When it rains, she ties a string of umbrellas to his body in an attempt to keep him dry. She takes advantage of his build at times, using him as a clothesline, or as an outdoor watchdog (Lengthy wraps himself around the whole house!)

He is a sensitive dog. He feels terrible that the nice old lady can't find enough money to buy the wool to knit him a sweater. Seeing that he is a financial burden, he runs away.

Lengthy goes to a rich neighborhood and is taken in by a wealthy family. He is treated very well, and he is introduced to all the best dogs. Nevertheless, he misses the poor old lady and decides to return home. On the way, Lengthy stumbles across a bank robbery. Or rather, the bank robbers stumble over Lengthy. He trips up their crime in progress, and receives a reward of five bags of money.

The dog carries the money home to the old lady, who now has enough capital to buy wool for two sweaters—one for the dog and one for herself.

This is an impossible story to adapt to puppets because of the exaggerated length of the dog. The pictures are large and clear and make puppet involvement unnecessary. But it is a fine fit with music! Since Lengthy marches around town so much—running away from home, circling the house, foiling the bank robbery, and so on, why not use a classical march with the story? Mozart's ever-popular "Turkish March" provides some cheerful traveling music. The correct name of the piece is "Rondo alla Turca," although it is widely known by its popular name. Many children will recognize this because it is standard piano lesson repetoire.

This piece could be used with any number of stories involving a good deal of marching, walking, or running. It is infectiously melodic and upbeat, and it whisks a story from one place to another very effectively.

Although Hoff's Lengthy is an exaggerated character, he shows the traits which endear so many dogs to humans: loyalty, affection, and protectiveness among them. This leads to a natural tie-in with some faithful dogs represented in art works.

If you can find a book on Norman Rockwell, you will almost certainly find his famous *Looking Out to Sea* (1919), which depicts an old man, a young boy, and a dog all gazing out at the vast sea before them. Fred Bauer's book, *The Faith of America*, illustrated by Rockwell, offers that plus another famous dog painting, *No Swimming*, in which boys and their loyal dog are running excitedly away from someone who has just discovered them frolicking in the water by the "No Swimming" sign.

For an art project, you could ask the children to draw a picture of themselves with their pet (or with the pet they would like to have). For a writing project or conversation topic, have the children tell a story about themselves and a pet.

✳ ✳ ✳

Here's another lovable dog story, this one from Nancy Carlson: *Harriet and Walt*. Although they are dogs, Harriet and Walt exhibit very human characteristics.

Harriet gets excited when she sees that it has begun to snow. She bundles up to run out and play, but her mother tempers Harriet's joy by reminding her to take her young brother Walt along.

Harriet digs a tunnel through a snowdrift, but Walt accidentally caves it in by crawling on top. Harriet makes a snow angel by lying on her back and moving her arms and legs back and forth. When she urges Walt to try it, the youngster lies face *down* in the snow.

Loudmouth George, Harriet's rabbit friend, asks her to play tag. They tell Walt to wait by the metal flagpole, but not to lick it. Of course, the first thing Walt does is get his tongue frozen to the metal. After many such incidents, George says Walt is really dumb. Harriet defends her young brother, and heads home.

On the way, she shows Walt how to make a snow angel, how to build a snowman without knocking it over, and how to sled. When their mother asks if they had a good time, Harriet explains that they did indeed—at least once they got rid of Loudmouth George.

These are all incidents that puppets can mime behind the storyteller. An occasional handful of book packing material (styrofoam or shredded paper) can be thrown over the stage to represent snow—and that always gets some giggles of delight.

Since this story is humorous from start to finish, I like to use some music that matches by featuring a humorous-sounding instrument. It is very difficult, for example, for a bassoon to sound extremely serious or profound.

Mozart's "Bassoon Concerto in B-flat" bubbles over with liveliness and good humor. The opening *Allegro* movement makes a nice combination with the antics of Harriet and Walt. The peppy and laughable sound of the bassoon goes nicely with the image of poor Walt flapping his legs as he makes a snow angel face down!

∗ ∗ ∗

Beverly Cleary's 1961 story, *Two Dog Biscuits*, centers around four-year-old twins, Jimmy and Janet, who are presented with two dog biscuits by the owner of a dog named Muffy, who lives next door.

The whimsical gift causes some problems, however. Their mother tells the children not to eat the biscuits because they are strictly for dogs. She suggests that the kids give them to Muffy, but they insist that Muffy has plenty.

Mother suggests a possible solution. She and Jimmy and Janet all set out for a walk around the neighborhood, in search of a nice dog to give the biscuits to.

They meet up with a big brown dog, but the children do not want to give their treats to either a big dog or a brown dog.

They meet a little white dog with an annoying "yip," and so they pass by this small nuisance.

They meet a big black dog with a loud bark and decide he is not deserving either. A number of other dogs meet the same rejection.

Finally they spot a calico cat and decide to offer it the dog biscuits. Mother thinks they will be too hard for the cat's teeth, but the cat shows some interest and starts nibbling on Janet's biscuit. The family watches in fascination as the cat eventually eats the whole thing and comes back for Jimmy's.

Throughout this story there is an interaction between the twins—both putting their dog biscuits in the same place, both dropping the treats out of their clothes as they get undressed for bed, both not liking the various dogs, both becoming intrigued by the prospect of feeding the cat. I thought of using music with a similar interaction between twin instruments and decided on the cheerful and playful opening movement of Mozart's "Concerto for Two Pianos."

The third movement (*Rondo*) seems well suited both in the sprightly mood and in the interplay of the duo-pianists. It has been said that Mozart probably composed the two piano pieces for himself and his sister, Nannerl. This would be one more reason to try it with Cleary's brother-sister book.

This story lends itself well to drawing and cutting out posterboard characters (the twins, parents, dogs, and one cat), mounting them on rods (the stiff cardboard bottoms of some coat hangers, or the wire parts, bent to fit, for example), and letting many children be "in" the story as you read it.

✻ ✻ ✻

Have you ever tried to look your very best for a photograph and found the picture to be embarrassingly silly? Such is the plight of Harry, the dog in Kathy Caple's *Harry's Smile*.

Harry dresses up in his Sunday best (which can be a cute scene to do with a puppet or stuffed dog), and goes off to have his portrait professionally done. He sits in front of the camera just a bit self-consciously, and he smiles as if he were a millionaire or a movie star.

The result is a silly-looking batch of pictures of a dog pretending to be someone he is not. Harry is so humiliated that he writes to his friend Wilma that he can no longer be her pen-pal, and he cannot send a photograph. He also refuses to smile ever again, even during a funny movie with his pal Sam. Sam tells amusing riddles and slurps his spaghetti, but he still can't make Harry smile.

Sam decides that it's time to take some drastic action. He contacts Wilma and asks her to come over. Wilma brings a camera, snaps a picture of Harry, and tells him that he looks great. Harry's humiliation melts away. The three friends are happy again, so they go to the park and ride the merry-go-round.

This story lends itself very well to having puppets and stuffed animals help the storyteller. Your volunteers will have a field day with sound effects, such as Sam's slurping his spaghetti and laughing at his own riddle, and Harry's moaning and wailing when he sees his silly photograph.

For music, George Gershwin's infectiously humorous and cheerful piano piece, "Rialto Ripples," is perfect throughout. This is the music that zany comedian Ernie Kovacs used frequently on his show in the early days of television and for good reason: it is undeniably silly.

For an art project, you could take off on the theme of smiles. If someone asked you what is the most famous smile in the history of art, you would probably say, the *Mona Lisa*. Leonardo da Vinci's famous painting is available in many framed picture collections in libraries and in innumerable books. Another good smile is Murillo's *A Girl and Her Duenna*. This captures the lady in the midst of suppressing a giggle and smile. It also appears in many art books. Other famous smiles in art can be found in Elizabeth Chase's *Famous Paintings*. They include Franz Hals's *The Laughing Cavalier* and *The Fisher Girl*, and Hogarth's *The Shrimp Girl*.

Try having the children draw different kinds of smiles. You can pass out paper with drawings of faces that have eyes, noses, and ears, but no mouths. Then ask the children first to draw a "silly" smile, and then maybe a "sneaky" smile and any other kinds of smiles you can think of!

✳ ✳ ✳

Ezra Jack Keats's practically wordless story *Pssst! Doggie* is based on a very simple premise: a cat asks a dog to dance, and they do.

Together the dog and cat dress up in costumes (a puppeteer who can sew could do more with this costume business than I can!). The puppets will dance to sea ditties, African music, Greek music, tap, Russian tunes, ballet music, French songs, and American colonial tunes.

This simple story represents a real challenge to anyone trying to orchestrate it! You'll need to create your own soundtrack, but the exposure your audience will get to different kinds of music is worth every effort.

For a sea dance, try a little of "The Sea and Sinbad's Ship" from Rimsky-Korsakov's *Scheherazade*. For a creative twist on the African dance, I use an authentic C.D. recording, *African Tribal Music and Dances*. Take your pick from the selections. For a Greek dance, try a traditional Greek folk tune. I use a piece called "Thessalonika Lou," from an album called *Greek Party*.

In another nontraditional match, for the tap dance segment I bring out Harry James's trademark swing trumpet tune "Ciribiribin", but any number of swing music selections could work just as well. For a few bars of authentic and danceable Russian music, how about the opening of "Sabre Dance" by Khachaturian? That will liven up things in a hurry.

For ballet music, any is fine, but I've used some of the many tuneful parts of "Coppelia" by Leo Delibes with good effect. And for lively French dance music for our two puppets, Offenbach's famous "Can-Can" is the undisputed favorite. Last of all, Sousa's "Washington Post March" works well for a colonial American dance background.

To make your soundtrack, just use ten or fifteen seconds from each of these pieces; otherwise it becomes too long. You can see how this variety of music provides differing backgrounds for all kinds of dance steps for your puppets. These "soundtrack stories" take quite a bit of time and effort to prepare, but they are fun!

✳ ✳ ✳

There is a wonderful series of Buster the Dog books available, which originated in Japan a few years ago. Before Patricia Lauber translated them and named the dog "Buster," the fluffy little puppy with the bell on his collar was called *Korowan*, by his creator, Hisako Madokoro, and painted by illustrator Ken Kuroi. My favorite of this charming, gentle series is *Buster Catches a Cold*, formerly known in Japanese as *Ame No Hi No Korowan*, which means *Korowan in the Rain*.

The origin of these stories gives us a good reason to bring a large map or globe into our storytelling session and point out a route by sea from the United States to Japan, identifying other countries along the way. Such a free geography lesson makes the stories more interesting. Already the children are given the concept that people all the way around the other side of the world are making up stories to be told to children like themselves.

At any rate, if you would like some puppets behind you for Korowan—that is, *Buster Catches a Cold*—you will need a dog, its mother, a frog, a snail, and, as long as you don't have a valuable Oriental rug in your story room, a large glass or two of water.

This particular story is very good for Florida, and other rainy areas, because the visual effects outside the window often fit the raininess of the story. It is pouring, but Buster feels (dog-) house bound and asks his mother if he may be allowed out. She says no, explaining that he might well catch a cold out in the rain. Buster is disappointed.

Mama Dog falls asleep, however, and Buster tells himself that it would be okay to go out, as long as he is careful that, if he SEES a cold, he makes sure not to CATCH it. Armed with that rationalization, Buster leaves the sanctuary of the dog house. Soon he realizes he is lacking one vital bit of information: Buster has no idea what a cold looks like. He meets a green creature which says "Rib-it," and he asks if it is a cold. The amused frog identifies itself to the puppy, and the two play tag in the rain.

The next unknown creature Buster encounters pops its head out of a shell. Again Buster asks if this strange creature might be a cold. After an explanation of snailhood, the two swim in the rain puddles. Later, Buster wonders if the colds might live in the puddles themselves. Finding a large puddle, Buster bravely peers in, and sees an ugly, wiggly face reflecting up at him. THAT must be a cold, he surmises, hitting the ugly creature with his paw and causing a terrific splash.

Buster starts to sneeze. Sure enough, his mother scolds him when he returns home. He caught a cold in the rain. No, Buster counters, he didn't even SEE a cold, much less CATCH one. But he did enjoy playing in the rain. (For another story of a dog with a cold, see *Henry and Mudge Get the Cold Shivers* by Cynthia Rylant in chapter 3.)

What a gentle, humorous story, with equally gentle, simple illustrations! The task in finding music to use with all the Buster stories, as I see it, is not necessarily to find something Japanese, but to find something consistently quiet, goodnatured, and orderly. Eventually I found a perfect match for the emotional tone of all the stories. It doesn't matter a bit that the music comes from Austria, or that the musicians come from France! Franz Joseph Haydn's *Six Flute Quartets* is consistently perfect throughout any part of the tape. Jean Pierre Rampal supplies the flute, accompanied by the chamber musicians from the Trio à Cordes Français.

Since Buster himself comes from Japan, we can also show some Japanese artwork. Tawaraya Sotatsu's *The Waves at Matushima* from the art book, *The Eastern Gate; An Invitation to the Arts of China and Japan* by Janet Gaylord Moore, shows waves depicted much like the rain in *Buster Catches a Cold*: decorative, simple, dramatic, and orderly. From the same book Ogata Korin's *Irises and Bridge* shows a Japanese rendering of flowers—simplified, somewhat abstract, always orderly and crisp.

Your particular library may not have my particular Japanese art book, but whatever you have will do just as well. Also, you may not have Haydn's flute quartets handy, but may find some other Haydn piece—or something of the same emotional tone from Mozart or Boccherini or a composer you may know. I recently caught the last movement of Mozart's final piano concerto on the radio and noted to myself that if I ever buy it, that would go very well with the Buster stories.

Another art form you can bring in here is haiku. The children's book *A Few Flies and I: Haiku by Issa* selected by Jean Merrill and Ronni Solbert, can help here. As Merrill explains in her introduction, in haiku only one thing happens. The poet tells of one event, one feeling, one movement. Haiku is compared to a little telegram and it takes the form of three lines consisting of five, seven, and five syllables.

> Soaking wet canine
> But not a whisker wiser
> Says he knows no colds.

How about reading a few good ones from a haiku book to the kids? (Children younger than fourth grade are probably too young for this complicated activity, although they might enjoy the simple poetry). Then you could pass out paper and ask them to create a haiku (or any poem) about the stories, or about how they feel. Pick your own topics.

As an example of subjects, you can mention that Issa wrote 54 haiku on the snail alone, 15 on toads, 200 on frogs, 230 on fireflies, 150 on flies, 100 on fleas, 90 on cicada, and 70 on miscellaneous other insects. That ought to give them some idea for subject matter they can use!

✳ ✳ ✳

My second favorite in the Buster series is *Buster's First Thunderstorm*. In this one, Buster and his dog friend, Snapper, are playing outdoors when a menacing storm starts creeping up on the horizon. Snapper is scared and leaves for home. Lonesome Buster asks some chicks if they would like to play, but they too are heading for a safe haven, at the urging of their mother. The desperate dog tries asking some ants to play, but they are also marching home.

Two butterflies, caught in the rain, lightning, and thunder which soon arrive, are being buffeted about in the wind. Buster offers quickly to let them grab onto the underside of his ample belly. The grateful butterflies hitch a ride on the taxi dog, all the way back to his dry, safe doghouse. When the sunshine and a rainbow come forth after the storm, Buster again plays outside with his two new friends.

If you use puppets with this one, there are some interesting opportunities to get creative. For the butterflies, I used butterfly-shaped refrigerator door magnets, taped to the tip end of coat hangers. We shook some sheets of construction paper to simulate the sounds of thunder and we used a tambourine to sound like lightning. Again, we're fond of hurling paper cups of water through the air to show the sudden rain (and add an element of surprise. See chapter 7). You can, if you have the time, staple some construction paper together in the shape of a rainbow and paint on the "vibgyor" colors (violet, indigo, blue-green, yellow, orange, and red.)

✳ ✳ ✳

In *Buster and the Little Kitten*, our good-hearted hero finds a lost kitten and magnanimously offers to help find its mother. Buster makes a few mistakes along the way. An orange cat hisses at him and tells him in no uncertain terms that she has no kittens. Buster bumps into an unfriendly gray cat who tells him to watch where he's going. Finally the mother is found and Buster returns home with a smile on his face.

An interesting international twist can be added here by introducing the children (and probably the parents) to the paintings of artist Carl Larsson. Larsson is like a Swedish version of Norman Rockwell. His cheerful, colorful, realistic depictions of his wife, children, pets, farm animals, home, neighbors, and countryside are treasured in museums, not only in his native Stockholm, but all over the world. It is a sad commentary on our education system, but I don't think I've ever shown these paintings to a child who had previously seen them or heard of Carl Larsson.

An animal-loving patron once pointed out to me the great number of cats and dogs tucked away in the nooks and crannies of Larsson's paintings. After a story like *Buster and the Little Kitten*, it's fun to take a collection such as *The Paintings of Carl Larsson*, edited by David Larkin, and ask the kids to try to find the cats and dogs. There's a cat warming itself by the stove in *The Kitchen: Suzanne and Kersti Churning Butter* (1900), and a cat hidden inside the barn in *Milking* (1905), and yet another near *The Gate* (1900). There are dogs blending in at *A Pleasant Bathing Place* (1900), and on *The Veranda* (1900), and at the *Open Air Breakfast* (1910–13), to name a few.

In case anyone thinks it's unusual to bring Carl Larsson into children's programming, do you remember George Mendoza's picture book from 1975, *Norman Rockwell's Americana ABC*? Nearly twenty years ago, an entire ABC book for the youngest of children was built entirely around the paintings of Norman Rockwell. So my suggestion is not unprecedented, especially with the similarities between Larsson and Rockwell.

The last three Buster books in the series all have something in common, especially if you're a puppeteer who loves to inject an occasional element of chaos (I should say "surprise," but that may be a little euphemistic).

I first tried using a large electric fan in back of a puppet stage several years ago—once—while telling *Curious George Goes to School*. When George turned on a fan and blew the children's artwork all over the classroom, we also turned loose a stack of papers in front of our own fan. It was a totally unexpected happening for the kids watching an otherwise predictable puppet show.

Well, just in case you get the urge, the last three Buster books also offer a chance to try an electric fan. In *Buster's First*

Snow, you can blow a box full of shredded paper to simulate the falling snow. In *Buster's Blustery Day,* you can let fly with a box of leaves. In *Buster and the Dandelions* you can blow off some flower petals or paper to simulate the dandelion "parachutes."

If you don't want to bother with a fan, of course, your puppeteers can simply throw things around by hand. It is worth noting that the element of surprise really is one of the cornerstones in the art of puppetry. I've written a whole chapter on it—see chapter 7.

How's that for an international story session? An Americanized dog from Japan, an American adapter, an Austrian composer, French musicians, Japanese artists, Japanese haiku, a Swedish artist, and a little American zaniness involving an electric fan! Buster has given us a chance to bring all kinds of elements together in one big (and fun) multicultural stew!

If you have a nice large world map handy, you also have a chance to point out where all these places are. We can do our part to clear up some of those notorious geography misconceptions American children are said to have.

A Sample Arts-Related Story Hour Program
Theme: Dogs, Cats, and Smiles
Ages preschool and early elementary

1. *Song*

    "Where, Oh Where Has My Little Dog Gone?" The story-teller leads the children in singing. An assistant works a dog puppet in and out from behind the stage's curtain.
2. *Musical story*

    Story: *Two Dog Biscuits* (Beverly Cleary)

    Music: "Concerto for Two Pianos" (third movement *Rondo*) (Mozart)

    Musical mood: Captures the cheerful interplay of the two twins.
3. *Activity*

    Draw some children and dog characters on poster board, cut them out, and mount them on rods. Hand out puppets and stuffed dogs (and one cat) so some children can be "in" the story as you tell it.
4. *Musical story*

    Story: *Harry's Smile* (Kathy Caple)

    Music: "Rialto Ripples" (George Gershwin)

    Musical mood: Sprightly, comical, good-humored.
5. *Art*

    Mona Lisa (da Vinci)

    A Girl and Her Duenna (Murillo)
6. *Drawing*

    Have children draw in different kinds of smiles—silly, sneaky, etc., on faces with no mouths.

References

Books:

Bauer, Fred. *The Faith of America.* Illustrated by Norman Rockwell. Abbeville Press, 1988.

Caple, Kathy. *Harry's Smile*. Houghton Mifflin, 1987.
Carlson, Nancy. *Harriet and Walt*. Carolrhoda, 1982.
Chase, Elizabeth. *Famous Paintings*. Platt and Munk, 1962.
Cleary, Beverly. *Two Dog Biscuits*. Dell, 1987.
Harold, Margaret. *Paintings by the Masters*. Allied Publications, 1966.
Hoff, Syd. *Lengthy*. G.P. Putnam's Sons, 1964.
Keats, Ezra Jack. *Pssst! Doggie*. Franklin Watts, 1973.
Larkin, David, ed. *The Paintings of Carl Larsson*. Bantam Books, 1976.
Madokoro, Hisako. Trans. by Patricia Lauber. *Buster and the Dandelions*. Gareth Stevens, 1991.
————. *Buster's Blustery Day*. Gareth Stevens, 1991.
————. *Buster Catches a Cold*. Gareth Stevens, 1991.
————. *Buster's First Snow*. Gareth Stevens, 1991.
————. *Buster's First Thunderstorm*. Gareth Stevens, 1991.
Mendoza, George. *Norman Rockwell's Americana ABC*. Dell, 1975.
Merrill, Jean, ed. *A Few Flies and I: Haiku by Issa*, selected by Jean Merrill and Ronni Solbert. Pantheon Books, 1969.
Moore, Janet Gaylord. *The Eastern Gate; An Invitation to the Arts of China and Japan*. William Collins, 1979.
Rey, Margret and Alan J. Shalleck, eds. *Curious George Goes to School*. Adapted from The Curious George Film Series. Houghton Mifflin, 1989.

Cassettes:

Haydn, Franz Joseph. *The Six Flute Quartets*. Seraphim 4XG–60327.
Mozart, Wolfgang. "Ronda alla Turca" ("Turkish March"). *Song Without Words: Fifteen Best Loved Piano Melodies*. London. 414 012–4.

Compact Discs:

African Tribal Music and Dances. Legacy International. 328.
Rimsky-Korsakov, Nikolai. "The Sea and Sinbad's Ship." *Scheherazade*. Leonard Bernstein and the New York Philharmonic Orchestra. CBS MYK–38476.

Record Albums:

Delibes, Leo. "Coppelia" *The Best of Ballet.* Westminster WGS–8136.

Gershwin, George. "Rialto Ripples." *Piano Music of W.E.A.* (Werner-Electra-Atlantic) 9019.

The Hellenes. "Thessalonica Lou." *Greek Party.* Tifton International TS 77.

James, Harry. "Ciribiribin." *Harry James in Hi Fi.* Capitol, EAP 1–654.

Khachaturian, Aram. "Sabre Dance." *Hi Fi Hits in Popular Classics.* Volume 1. Westminster XWN—18888.

Mozart, Wolfgang. "Bassoon Concerto in B flat Major." *Mozart Music for Winds and Brass.* Murray Hill. S–4364.

————. "Concerto for Two Pianos in E flat Major." Vitya Vronsky and Victor Babin, duo-pianists. E.M.I. Angel G7152.

Offenbach, Jacques. "Can-Can." *The Lure of France.* Columbia CS 8111.

Rimsky-Korsakov, Nikolai. "The Sea and Sinbad's Ship." *Scheherazade.* London PM 55002.

Sousa, John Philip. "Washington Post March." *Semper Fidelis - The Marches of John Philip Sousa.* Harmony HL 7001.

10
Stories That Tug at the Heart

There are certain stories that may well bring a tear to the eye, and these sensitive books deserve an equally sensitive choice of musical background.

One such book is Kathryn O. Galbraith's *Laura Charlotte* with moving illustrations by Floyd Cooper. In this very touching book, Little Laura asks her mother to tell her a bedtime story (the usual one) about how her stuffed elephant came into their possession. Laura's great-grandmother had originally made the elephant from gray flannel scraps. Laura's grandmother passed it down to Laura's mother, who loved it, but accidentally left it outside, and a cat tore its ear. Charlotte the Elephant—so named because that was the "prettiest name in the world"—was taken to Mom's grandmother for repair of the ear. When Laura's mom grew up and married, she kept Charlotte in a box for the child she hoped to have someday. That child was named Laura after the grandmother, and Charlotte, because it was still the prettiest name in the world. The last illustration shows the four generations together with the stuffed elephant.

I'm not at all sure I can describe the exceptional ability the author and illustrator have to move people with this text and its pictures. In looking for a piece of music to match this emotional power I found the "Intermezzo" from Bizet's *Carmen Suite. Carmen* was first staged in 1875. Fifteen years later, Tchaikovsky said it would become the most popular opera in the world. Time has certainly not changed the accuracy of that prediction very much.

✳ ✳ ✳

Another touching story combining the poetic sensitivity of a writer with the brilliant interpretation of an illustrator is Nancy White Carlstrom's *Wild, Wild Sunflower Child, Anna*, with illustrations by Jerry Pinkney. This book poetically follows Anna as she runs and jumps through fields of flowers; picks raspberries; hops from rock to rock in the creek; climbs trees and hills; dances and daydreams in the meadow; watches ants, beetles, and spiders; and sleeps in the sunflowers.

Let's stay with the *Carmen Suite* for the music. If you saw the movie, *Flashdance*, you may remember a scene in which Jennifer Beals, the actress who played the dancer, crosses a busy street with a policeman directing traffic in all directions. The scene is set to "Le Garde Montante," a brief but charming movement from the *Carmen Suite*. Beals's lighthearted mimicry of the policeman and their waves to each other become a humorous ballet as she dances across the street. The music also goes very well with Anna's dancing and jumping and rolling and hopping in this book. It would indeed go well with any book full of movement or marching or parading. It's thoroughly alive and delightful — just like the wild sunflower child, Anna.

You couldn't find a more natural art tie-in than a reproduction of Van Gogh's *Sunflowers*. This is available in framed versions in library collections as well as in most books on Van Gogh, and other art books such as Elizabeth Chase's *Famous Paintings*. It is probably the most popular painting of flowers ever done.

For a drawing or painting project, ask the children to look more closely at flowers in both book and painting. A box of plastic flowers from a discount store, or even more "flowery" and expensive silk ones, are one of the most useful props for any number of stories. Have the children try to draw them either in a realistic way, like Pinkney, or an imaginative and expressionistic way, like Van Gogh.

✳ ✳ ✳

In our community here in South Florida, Eve Bunting's *How Many Days to America?* is an especially poignant story. As I write this, the morning paper informs us that thirty-nine or more Haitian refugees drowned at sea while fleeing in an overcrowded boat for the promised land in Miami. Bunting's book likewise is about a boatload of refugees from an unnamed island in the Caribbean, escaping from a military force they do not agree with. Scenes like this have been played out a lot recently in Florida, and the story may help to educate children from other areas who do not really understand the precarious existence of refugee peoples.

On the ocean the families are robbed by some armed men from another boat. They are also sent away from one landing spot. They survive on papayas, lemons, and coconuts until they reach the Florida shores. Here they celebrate Thanksgiving with other refugees, in a shed with a tin roof. They give thanks as they start their new lives.

We need music which is both poignant and thematic for this special story. I use the famous *Largo* movement of Dvorak's *Symphony no. 5*, "From the New World." It is specifically about immigration to the New World, so there is a certain kindredness of spirit between the music and the story. You're probably familiar with the poignancy of this melody, as it was popularized in 1922 as a song, "Goin' Home," with lyrics by William Arms Fisher.

An excellent tie-in with art here is provided by Norman Rockwell's four paintings, *The Four Freedoms*, which were started in 1941. These were inspired by an address President Franklin Delano Roosevelt gave to Congress at that time. FDR spoke of freedom of speech, freedom of worship, freedom from want, and freedom from fear as the four essential human freedoms. Rockwell painted a man speaking his mind at a meeting, people in prayer, a family at a home Thanksgiving dinner to represent the first three. The final painting representing freedom from fear depicts a mother and father tucking their children in bed, while the father is holding a newspaper at his side with some frightening headlines.

For older children—at least second graders—a teacher or storyteller could mention the first amendment of the Bill of Rights at this point, touching on freedom of religion, speech, assembly, and the press. Explain what a "right" means and does not mean. People have a right to express opinions, for example— but that doesn't mean kids can babble away through a class or storytime! (This is usually a meaningful distinction, and will get you a laugh). Ask the children to offer their ideas of what a "right" is.

❋ ❋ ❋

Another picture book depicting life of children from an unnamed place—most likely Jamaica—is Juanita Havill's *Jamaica Tag-Along*.

This story is basically about children's feelings. Jamaica is a girl about ten years old. She has nothing to do on a particular day, so she asks her older brother Ossie if she can go with him to play basketball with the boys. He says no, but she tags along anyway. She even grabs the ball when it comes her way, causing a great uproar among the boys, who banish her unceremoniously to the swings. Her feelings are hurt.

After a while, Jamaica starts to build a sand castle in the sand lot. A bored preschooler named Berto comes along, fascinated by the castle, and announces that he will help. He clumsily knocks down a wall, causing Jamaica to shoo him away.

Berto's mother tells him that big kids don't like to be bothered by little kids. Jamaica realizes that this is exactly what Ossie said to her, and she remembers how badly she felt. She therefore has a change of heart and invites Berto to come back. She teaches him how to build the castle and not knock over walls.

Finally Ossie comes by after his basketball game. He sees the castle and wants to join in the fun. Jamaica good naturedly lets Ossie "tag along." We're not sure how this will affect Jamaica's status at boys' basketball games in the future, but for the moment, at least, we have an intergenerational harmony. Children reading or listening to it will become a little more aware of the feelings of their own brothers and sisters, and of other children's feelings as well.

Caribbean steel drum music—such as "Mary Ann" from *Beautiful Barbados*—can create an islands background mood for this story. Have the children write or tell about times their own feelings were hurt.

✳ ✳ ✳

Daydreamers by Eloise Greenfield, with illustrations by Tom Feelings, is another very sensitively done book in every respect. Tom Feelings has garnered many awards for his book illustrations, including the Coretta Scott King award. and Caldecott Honor Book awards. When you see his drawings of African-American children, with an equally profound text by Eloise Greenfield, you will surely understand why he has been so honored.

This is a book to be read to a small group only, so they can enjoy the illustrations. There's nothing puppets could add to these. The pictures need to be seen. We can, however, add some dreamy background music with great success. Pieces such as Stephen Foster's "Beautiful Dreamer" (orchestral version) fit very nicely with the mood of this beautiful book. Debussy's "Reverie" is another.

Dreams have found their way into art. Marc Chagall's *The Dream* (1939), for example, reflects well the topsy-turvy, mixed-up nature of dreaming. The bed with people in it is outdoors, surrounded by an angel, a rooster, and jumbled houses. This painting can be found in *Chagall—Watercolors and Gouaches* by Alfred Werner. Another painting from the same book, called *Reverie* (1931) depicts a figure reclining in a chaise lounge in the midst of some alpine mountain scenery.

Having the children try their hand at drawing a dream, or writing a story about a dream or just talking about dreams can be a lively and expressive experience.

✳ ✳ ✳

Julie Brinckloe's picture book, *Fireflies*, will bring waves of nostalgia to anyone who has ever run through the streets as a child with a jar for capturing fireflies. I know it reminds me a whole lot of nights we did that as kids in Philadelphia.

The illustrations by Ms. Brinckloe capture the excitement of seeing these lightning bugs blinking on and off, both in the air and in the jars. There is something phenomenal about these special events, capturing creatures which make moonlight in a jar.

In fact, the book reminds me of quite a few things. The boy in the story lives in a two-story brick house with steps going down to the cellar, where jars are stored. So did I. All the kids run for their jars excitedly and roam the streets in groups. So did we.

At night the boy lies in his bed for a long time watching his fireflies. Eventually their lights grow dim and they fall to the bottom of the jar. Seeing this, the boy takes the jar to the window, unscrews the lid which has small holes punched through it, and hurls the fireflies back into the open air. They begin to perk up and brighten the sky again, as they fly off into the dark night. This Junior Literary Guild selection captures the magic of the entire experience.

I ventured a little from my usual repertoire in order to find music for this one. I settled on jazz/classical trumpeter Wynton Marsalis for his show-stopping rendition of Paganini's "Perpetual Motion." When you listen to this particular piece you'll find yourself wondering, "When does he breathe?" It is indeed nonstop perpetual motion (or perpetual sound), and it certainly creates an appropriate background for fast, flickering fireflies.

The only problem with trumpet music is that it doesn't always stay in the background as harp and flute music do. If you don't keep the volume down pretty low on this one it can overwhelm the storyteller—particularly with this quiet, sensitive story.

∗ ∗ ∗

Music, Music for Everyone by Vera Williams is a picture book that will also tug at the heartstrings. The little girl at the center of the story plays the accordion and takes music lessons at school along with her friends. Leora plays the drums, Jenny plays the "fiddle" (violin), and Mae plays the flute. Without a word, we see from the illustrations already that this is both a quietly interracial and intergenerational story. The various races and generations are at ease together and thoroughly enjoy each other.

Grandma and Mama sit together in a huge red-rose patterned chair to listen to the girl play the accordion. The music reminds Grandma of her village home long ago, and she loves to clap along with it.

Grandma suddenly becomes ill, however, and has to stay upstairs in bed. Mama often makes soup and the girl carries it upstairs to her grandmother, where she sits on the bed and fills Grandma in on all the family's and neighbors' doings.

The other children from the music class notice how empty the house is without the grandmother downstairs. They also notice that the family money jar seems rather empty and they figure that the family must be dipping into it heavily to meet the expenses of the grandmother's illness. Leora mentions that her own family's money jar was low, too, when her father had an accident and couldn't go to work. Mae even puts a dime into the jar.

The little girl's other grandmother had played the accordion, too, at parties and weddings. The child wonders if she could do the same—and earn money to help out. Her sick grandmother expresses total confidence in the girl's ability to do this, and the idea for a small children's band begins to form.

After a good deal of consultation and practice with the school music teacher, the Oak Street Band is formed. Leora's mother gives the children their first paying job, playing at a party for Leora's great-grandparents. Everyone loves their music. After the party, Jenny falls asleep before deciding what to do with her profits; Mae is not sure; Leora saves hers for a bigger drum. The accordion girl, however, put her portion directly into the family money jar.

Recorded accordion music is not that easy to find, but anything else would be inappropriate for this story! I have an old *Myron Floren Accordion Concert* album which contains "Czardas" and "Lady of Spain," both of which have the sound and feel of the music described in this very rich and warm picture book. Polka music featuring an accordion would work nicely as well.

Artists have also been interested in capturing people's love of making music. In Robert Maillard's *History of Painting*, for instance, we find ancient Egyptian works such as *Women Making Music* with harps and other stringed instruments. This dates back to the Eighteenth Dynasty. More recently, Norman Rockwell painted *Shuffleton's Barbershop* for a 1950 *Saturday Evening Post* cover. This depicts a gathering of four locals playing various musical instruments in the back room of a barbershop. This can be found in *Norman Rockwell's America* by Christopher Finch.

A neat contrast here, and a way to introduce some modern art, is to show Picasso's *The Three Musicians* (1921). This very abstract painting is Picasso's unique depiction of a pianist, violinist, and flute player. It is found in H.W. Janson's *The Story of Painting*, as well as most books on Picasso and modern art.

The contrast between Rockwell's and Picasso's musicians gives us a chance to make an important point. Drawing or painting a person doesn't mean we have to make it look like a photographic likeness. We can be completely playful and use our imaginations, like Picasso, and use any colors and shapes we like—and still call it a picture of musicians. We can say that Picasso was more interested in the shapes and colors than in what the musicians really looked like. The children could say which type of drawing would be most fun for them if they were drawing the child next to them. They could try out either or both methods. Art, we can tell them, can be a lot of things.

✳ ✳ ✳

The First Doll in the World by Lee Pape takes us back to prehistoric times. In this book, we meet the little cave dweller, Twinkle, as she sweeps out the floor of the mountain home. She lives with her father, Hairy Man, and her mother, Tender Eyes. Her only friend is her pet, Big Brawn, the wolf dog.

Father is often out hunting. Mother is often roasting food over the open fire. There are no TVs to watch and no neighbor children to play with, so it is a lonely life for Twinkle, who occupies herself gathering nuts and listening to the songs of the birds.

(Here's an opportunity for puppets, with chirps from the puppeteers.)

Tender Eyes makes hats of leaves for her little girl. (This is something the puppeteer can get together as well, using leaves glued to a small hat. You may want to take the hat from one of the puppets and try it on a small girl in the audience, explaining how the leaves keep the hot sun off.) But Twinkle grows lethargic and sick, and the doctor's potion does nothing to cure her. She tells her dog that she needs something to love, to cuddle, to hold tight, to go to sleep with at night, and to play with in the day.

She does not have a name—like "doll"—for such a thing, for dolls don't exist. She can, however, use the universal language of art to draw such an object on the wall of the cave.

Tender Eyes instantly understands. She takes some twigs, fibers, reindeer fur, etc., and makes the first doll in the history of the world.

Our puppeteers could put together a similar doll to illustrate. The storyteller could bring out a modern doll to compare it with. The first doll can't blink its eyes, like today's dolls. Its hair isn't curled.It can't walk or talk or wet. Nevertheless, it serves its purpose perfectly.

A special story such as *The First Doll in the World* deserves some special music to go with it. How about the warm, lyrical, and melodious *Adante* (or second movement) of Mozart's "Elvira Madigan" concerto (Piano Concerto no. 21). This very familiar, very moving piece could be used with any number of stories which are tender and sensitive in nature.

This is a story with an unusual tie-in: prehistoric art. Many art books, such as Robert Maillard's *History of Painting*, have examples. This book shows the mineral color depictions of bison, horses, bulls, and cows in the Lascaux Cave (France) and Altamira Cave (Spain). It's certainly an interesting concept to teach children that early humans were creating art over 12,000 years ago!

For art participation, have the children draw their ideas of cave people. You can let them draw dinosaurs too, but be sure to explain that early humans and T-Rex did not co-exist! Then ask the children to write or talk about what they would be doing if they and their families lived in prehistoric times.

✳ ✳ ✳

Another heart tugger, especially for anyone with a younger brother or sister, is *Princess Pearl* by Nicki Weiss.

Pearl's big sister, Rosemary, is quite a bossy, domineering sort. Pearl always has to play what Rosemary wants, even if the younger girl is tired of play-acting "Sleeping Beauty." Not only that, Pearl is banned from their shared bedroom when Rosemary's friends come over.

When they fight—and Rosemary wins—the bigger sister sits on Pearl and licks her nose. More humiliation!

Finally, Rosemary puts a strip of tape down the middle of their bedroom floor, to ensure her privacy.

The situation changes dramatically, however, with a visit by Pearl's new friend, Janie Sachs. Rosemary, from her bed, hears Janie bragging about how she doesn't have to share her bedroom with anyone—and it's bigger, besides. Next, Janie refuses to play what Pearl enjoys. The last straw for Rosemary is when Janie decides to play dress up, with Janie being the princess and Pearl being the servant girl.

With a sudden surge of sisterly protectiveness, Rosemary storms across the divider tape, announces that Pearl will be the princess, and marches her off to help her dress! When Janie leaves, the two sisters are closer than they have ever been. Pearl likes her princess clothes so much that she decides to wear them to supper.

You could go off in various directions looking for background music for this one. You could pick something sweet and sentimental to use toward the end. Or you could use something humorous to accent the sibling rivalry. The title piece from *Feuding Banjos* certainly fits the theme of feuding sisters, and accentuates the humor as well!

In the art world, Thomas Gainsborough's *The Painter's Daughters* is an eighteenth-century portrait of his two daughters, one with her arms affectionately wrapped around her younger sister. This can be found in Michael Levey's *A Concise History of Painting*.

For writing or discussion, have the children tell a story about one of their own brothers or sisters, or perhaps about a good friend.

✳ ✳ ✳

Let's finish our tug-at-the-heart chapter with a Caldecott Award book, Karen Ackerman's *Song and Dance Man*, illustrated by Stephen Gammell.

In this story, Grandpa dusts off his old tap shoes with the silver half-moon taps from up in the family attic, along with his top hats and bow ties. The three children try on the costumes and take great delight in hearing Grandpa sing "Yankee Doodle." He also plays his old banjo while he sings—so that banjo music album mentioned in the past two stories could indeed be used again. However, we have other musical options, which I'll get to.

Grandpa sprinkles some powder on the floor and does a dance routine for the kids, who find this better than TV! He tells corny jokes and does magic tricks for his enthralled young audience as well. What a concept for the 1990s generation to discover—live entertainment!

Grandpa loved his vaudeville, but he says he wouldn't trade the time he now has with his grandchildren to go back and live in the past. That gives us a clue about Grandpa's priorities being in very good order.

I tried to find some appropriate vaudeville music to go with this book. I use "Me and My Shadow," which has long been a staple of song-and-dance stage routines. It's available in many collections: Lawrence Welk has one on his *All My Personal Favorites* album.

Perhaps you could ask some of the kids to come up front and dance to the music, for the rest of the audience. I always let the parents stay in the room for my preschool and early elementary story sessions. (The room holds over 200, so space is no problem.) In a classroom, there are generally kids who like to perform and kids who prefer to be the audience.

Stories That Tug at the Heart

A Sample Arts-Related Story Hour Program
Theme: Immigrants in America
Ages preschool and early elementary

1. *Musical story*

   Story: *How Many Days to America?* (Eve Bunting)

   Music: "Goin' Home". *Largo* movement, *Symphony no. 5,* "From the New World." (Dvorak)

   Musical mood: Poignant, expressive of being uprooted and relocated.

   Art: "The Four Freedoms" (Rockwell)

2. *Musical story*

   Story: *Jamaica Tag-Along* (Juanita Havill)

   Music: "Mary Ann," from *Beautiful Barbados—Steel Drums.* Madacy, MW–2015.

   Musical mood: Calypso, cheerfully reminiscent of Jamaica or other islands of the region.

   Writing or conversation topic: Tell about times your own feelings were hurt.

3. *Musical story*

   Story: *Music, Music for Everyone* (Vera Williams)

   Music: "Lady of Spain" or other accordion music

   Musical mood: Cheerful folk music evocative of "the old country"—somewhere in Europe, but not specified.

4. *Art*

   Women Making Music (ancient Egyptian)

   Shuffleton's Barbershop (Rockwell)

   The Three Musicians (Picasso)

5. *Activity*

   Ask the kids if anyone knows how to say certain words in other languages: "Hello," "Good morning," "friend," "book," etc. (If parents are present at a library story hour, they can help.) In South Florida, we have families from Haiti, Cuba, Pakistan, Korea, China, Japan—to name just a few!

111

References

Books:

Ackerman, Karen. *Song and Dance Man.* Knopf, 1988.
Brinckloe, Julie. *Fireflies.* Macmillan, 1985.
Bunting, Eve. *How Many Days to America? A Thanksgiving Story.* Clarion, 1988.
Carlstrom, Nancy White. *Wild, Wild Sunflower Child, Anna.* Macmillan, 1987.
Chase, Elizabeth. *Famous Paintings.* Platt and Munk, 1962.
Finch, Christopher. *Norman Rockwell's America.* Reader's Digest, 1975.
Galbraith, Kathryn O. *Laura Charlotte.* Philomel, 1990.
Greenfield, Eloise and Tom Feelings. *Daydreamers.* Dial, 1981.
Havill, Juanita. *Jamaica Tag-Along.* Houghton Mifflin, 1989.
Janson, H.W. *The Story of Painting.* Harry N. Abrams, 1966.
Levey, Michael. *A Concise History of Painting.* Praeger, 1962.
Maillard, Robert. *The History of Painting.* Tudor, 1961.
Pape, Lee. *The First Doll in the World.* Lothrop, Lee, and Shepard, 1961.
Weiss, Nicki. *Princess Pearl.* Greenwillow, 1986.
Werner, Alfred. *Chagall Watercolors and Gouaches.* Watson-Guptill, 1977.
Williams, Vera. *Music, Music for Everyone.* Greenwillow, 1984.

Cassettes:

Bizet, Georges. "Intermezzo." *Carmen Suite.* Philips. 411 175–4.
————. "Le Garde Montante." *Ibid.*
Marsalis, Wynton. *Wynton Marsalis—Carnaval.* Columbia 1MT 42137.
Mozart, Wolfgang Amadeus. "Piano Concerto no. 21" ("Elvira Madigan"—*Andante*, second movement). *Mozart: Piano Concertos 21 and 12.* Treasury, 417 685–4.

Record Albums:

Debussy, Claude. "Reverie." *The Lure of France.* André Kostalanetz and His Orchestra. Columbia CS 8111.

Dvorak, Antonin. Symphony no. 5, (From the New World"). Mercury Classics. MG 50002.

Feuding Banjos. "Saturday Night Banjo" and "Whistle While You Work" by Mason Williams; "Feuding Banjos" by Eric Weissberg and Marshall Brickman. Olympic Records. 7105.

Floren, Myron. *Myron Floren Accordion Concert as Featured on Lawrence Welk T.V. Shows.* Dot. DLP 3315.

Foster, Stephen. "Beautiful Dreamer." *The Wonderful World of Music.* (Side 17: Stephen Foster Melodies). Miller International Company. MO-TP–9A.

"Me and My Shadow." *All My Personal Favorites.* Lawrence Welk. Ranwood RLP 8183.

11

Relationships—
Families, Friends, Animals

There are many picture books about relationships between parents and children, between friends, relatives, teachers and children, or pets and children. One such, Eve Bunting's *The Wednesday Surprise*, is certainly a story about a special relationship, for in it a young girl teaches her grandmother how to read. They work secretly together on Wednesday nights, while the girl's mother works late and the father, a truckdriver, is on the road. They even manage to wolf down a little ice cream during these "literacy tutoring" sessions.

The book captures the joy of someone's learning to read. As the grandmother becomes more and more adept at reading, she and the child prepare to surprise the family at father's birthday party. After all the presents have been opened, the two announce the best present of all: Grandma reads *The Velveteen Rabbit* and other stories aloud. Father's eyes well up with tears. Mother is astonished. Grandma kids them that maybe now she'll read everything in the world. She has time, she says.

The relationships here are so loving between family members, we need music that can portray love and caring. There is much to choose from in classical or popular music, but Liszt's "Liebestraum no. 3" ("Dream of Love") captures the essence of these feelings as well as any. I use the sensitive piano version by Philippe Entremont. Beethoven's "Für Elise" is another good choice.

One of the more famous depictions of the pleasures of reading can be found in the *Forest of Fountainbleau*, a painting by Jean Baptiste Camille Corot. It depicts a verdant, lush deep woods, and down in the corner we find a young woman lying on the ground enjoying a good book in sumptuous solitude! This can be found in many library framed art collections, books on Corot, and art anthologies. It makes a nice tie-in to Bunting's book.

Another fitting piece of art is Norman Rockwell's *The Reading Hour*, which depicts Grandpa in a large chair smiling over at his granddaughter contentedly reading a book in a smaller chair. The girl is pointing out the words carefully with her right index finger.

An interesting writing topic, if the children in your story hour are old enough, is "What I remember about learning to read." If they're not that far along, you could talk about what they would like to read when they learn how to do so.

✳ ✳ ✳

Owl Moon, the Caldecott Medal winner by Jane Yolen, is another story of a strong relationship—this one between a man and child. Together they go owling in the dark night woods. The sounds they hear are only a lonesome train whistle, crunching snow, and the barking of dogs.

In the woods, the man attracts owls by imitating their calls. His flashlight illuminates the wild bird, making this "hunt" a success. The authenticity of the book comes from the fact that author Jane Yolen's husband took their children owling in rural Massachusetts, and illustrator John Schoenherr shared the owling experience with his own children—and used his own farm and familiar landmarks in the pictures he did for the book.

A good deal of first-hand bonding between parents and children went into this story.

I tried a very unusual recording with *Owl Moon*, Swiss mountain music called "Alphorn with Cattle Bells," because it evoked woods, mountains, and the wild. The opening movement of Beethoven's "Moonlight Sonata" would be much easier to locate and would serve just as well, but it was fun to try something very different.

✳ ✳ ✳

A Chair for My Mother by Vera B. Williams is about the special relationship between a mother and daughter, which expands to include relatives and caring neighbors. In this book, the mother is a waitress in the Blue Tile diner, and depends on tips to keep afloat financially. She lives with her daughter and her own mother in an apartment.

One day there is a terrible fire, and the apartment and the furniture are ruined. The three have to move in with relatives before they get another apartment. Neighbors bring pizza and ice cream. One gives them a table and three chairs. An old man gives them a bed from when his own children were little. An aunt makes curtains. The other grandma brings a rug. A cousin even gives the girl a stuffed bear. Everyone knows about the plight of these people due to the fire and they all rally around to help in any way they can.

The daughter feels badly that her mother comes home tired and has no easy chair or sofa to sit on and relax. A large jar is a visible sign of hope, however, as coins are diligently put in it, and after a long time enough is collected to buy the chair. Now mother and daughter can sit in the big, cozy chair together. Grandma can sit in it during the day and talk to neighbors out the window.

This is a very warm story of relationships between a real community of people—family, friends, and neighbors. It is a quiet story of people helping people in time of need, and of looking for ways to make life better for others. Author Vera Williams is also a graphic artist, and she captured the spirit of the story beautifully in her illustrations.

This is a very comforting and caring story, tinged with elements of fear and loss. Franz Schubert's music would be a good choice to accompany it. Schubert spent most of his short life living off the generosity of friends. Much of his music went unnoticed in his lifetime. The final movement of his "Unfinished Symphony" (Symphony no. 8) has those qualities of sweetness and pathos, a rather complex emotional mix to match the sweetness and sadness of the story.

Norman Rockwell provides another tie-in to a story here. For a painting which shows a neighborhood coming together, try *Homecoming G.I.* in *Norman Rockwell's America* by Christopher Finch. The soldier returning home from the war is greeted by family, neighbors in windows, kids in trees, an enthusiastic beagle dog, a turtle, a repairman on the porch roof and one shy girl waiting for the right and proper moment to greet the young soldier.

For a writing or talking topic, ask the children to think about get-togethers in their own neighborhood, or perhaps about times when their families were helped during hard times.

✳ ✳ ✳

The Lost Lake by Allen Say is the story of a father and his boy. Luke's parents are divorced and Luke has gone to live with his Dad in the summer. His father doesn't talk much and spends most of his time working at his drafting table—even on weekends.

Dad does manage to get five days off for a camping trip, however, and the two set off hiking in search of Lost Lake, where Grandpa used to take Luke's father when he was a youngster himself.

Luke enters the world of the woods a little reluctantly, but discovers, to his delight, that Dad is a different person out here—he talks more. He sees how disappointed Dad is when they discover that Lost Lake has become something of a tourist mecca, but they push deeper into the woods and mountains until finally they discover another lake—this one truly "lost." The two enjoy their tent, their own cooking, their discovery, and, most of all, each other's company.

I'll return to Schubert again for this story, only this time it's Schubert in a more robust mood. His "Impromptu no. 4" sounds very much like a tromp through the woods, and even evokes rippling streams and lakes. It does have the familiar Schubert harmonious quality, without the pathos, and is certainly appropriate for this outdoorsy story of a relationship happily deepening.

✳ ✳ ✳

Judith Viorst's *The Goodbye Book* is a more humorous look at a relationship—this time between a boy, his babysitter, and his parents.

This little boy is a terror. He throws an enormous fit when his parents hire a babysitter so they can go to a French restaurant. The boy wants them to take him to McDonald's instead. He is quite imaginative and vocal about the horrors of a babysitter: after all, the sitter might make him watch *her* TV show. Anyway, he's sick. He claims to have a temperature approaching 110 degrees. He even threatens to run away and find a new family.

All is well when he sees the babysitter, and she reads to him and plays with him. All his imaginings were for naught. We just hope the poor parents aren't having too much of a guilt trip at the French restaurant! They didn't seem overly concerned with the boy's tantrum when they kissed him good night, so it's probably safe to assume they're having a good time.

A couple of interesting combinations result from trying different musical backgrounds for this story. Falla's "Ritual Fire Dance" offers some wild, stomping rhythms that go as well with a temper tantrum as with a fire dance! Mendelssohn's "Song Without Words" is a piano piece which offers a staccato buzzing quality, with hundreds of notes quickly played, matching the mood of the buzzing, complaining little boy. Either one works well, depending on your preference.

✳ ✳ ✳

Jean Speare's *A Candle for Christmas* takes place on the Chilcotin Plateau in British Columbia, Canada, in the far-below-zero winter season. It is a story of relationships on an Indian reservation, between young Thomas, his family, and nurse Roberta.

For music, there are different ways you can go. If you choose to accentuate the sub-zero temperatures, you could bring out the final movement of the "Winter" section of *The Four Seasons* by

Vivaldi, mentioned in chapter 3. You could also find something to accentuate the warmth of the relationships rather than the coldness of the climate, such as the moving *Adagio* section of Mozart's "Concerto for Clarinet."

Back to our story. Thomas's parents set off on a two-week journey to find out if something is wrong with Uncle Alphonse on the cattle range. (Sure enough, he has broken a leg and wolves are killing the cattle.) Thomas is left at the reservation in the care of nurse Roberta. She provides the boy with a Christmas tree to decorate. Thomas lights a candle to see it by, and dreams the candle grows huge and leads his parents home. Nurse Roberta is called away to attend to a sick baby, so Thomas's loneliness intensifies. He brings wood in to keep the fire going inside the stove.

Finally his parents return—a week later then planned—with Uncle Alphonse and the cattle. The family rejoices that they have been reunited safely in time for Christmas. Jean Speare's text and illustrator Ann Blades's paintings capture the joy of being together for Christmas on this reservation, and the Dvorak music certainly adds to the feeling of Indian life and the ever-present Canadian winter.

Nancy Lou Patterson's book, *Canadian Native Art*, gives us a chance to show some authentic Indian pieces, such as the colorful "transformation mask" on the cover and on page 136. The central face is surrounded by composite animal and sea life. The mask suggests the dual animal-human nature of their ancestors, whose stories are re-enacted by dancers wearing masks. Our library children can relate to that idea as we often use masks in our storytelling (see chapter 8).

Such art, music, and stories can help teachers bring a unit on Indians to life, supplementing traditional texts.

✳ ✳ ✳

The Berenstain Bears and the Bad Dream explores relationships and also the causes and cures of bad dreams. It further makes a very good commentary on our many outer space horror movies.

Brother Bear loves to collect "Space Grizzlies," toy action figures of the monsters from the movies of that name. We've all seen these on TV or in theaters over the past decade—all the gruesome special effects and grotesque figures hurtling around space. They're certainly enough to give children nightmares—and in this book, they do!

Brother is so enraptured with the things, he does chores to earn money to buy more and more, including the spectacular "Sleezos Cloud Castle." Brother Bear walks dogs, carries in groceries, and does other odd jobs in order to raise money to purchase these toys. He even submits to a bribe to get his sister to play with these toys with him. He agrees to play her games of paper dolls, beanbag toss, and jacks.

That night, following their intergalactic shootout, Sister Bear wakes up screaming. Mama and Papa try to explain to her how dreams come about, and try to calm her down. They explain that people's brains keep working even after they fall asleep, and that all the things people have had on their minds come together in a way that doesn't make much sense, and can be scary.

Nightmares next hit Brother Bear, as the grizzlies come after him too in a bad dream. Sister Bear explains to him what their parents had told her about nightmares. We readers are left with a vivid picture of how commercialized violence can, and does, affect children. We also see family members trying to deal with a problem they were not aware of previously.

Earlier in this book the famous opening movement of Beethoven's "Moonlight Sonata" was used to create a mood of suspense and quiet mystery. For this story, we can use the less famous, far more frenetic third movement to portray the turmoil and scariness of the space grizzlies. The album notes I have refer to this movement as one of the first tumultous outpourings which Beethoven unleashed in these piano sonatas. The notes liken the movement to gigantic electrical flashes. This image gives you an idea of how well the music fits space grizzlies!

A story like this could certainly be used as a starting point for children to draw their own "Space Grizzlies" or scary monsters.

✳ ✳ ✳

Mercer Mayer's *Just Shopping with Mom* is a pretty realistic look at the relationships between a mother, son, daughter, and baby in a grocery store.

The younger sister is a personality type we've all probably encountered more than once. She demands to be pushed in the cart, along with the baby. Brother has to push not only the infant but his lump of a little sister too—and she is nearly as big as he is. She helps herself to a plum off the shelf; she begs for candy and books and a wooden yellow duck and a red pail. Being turned down just spurs her on to ask for more things.

Soon she is asking for ice cream, cake, another kitten, a doll. Mother explains that she needs a new dress instead, and they manage to buy one. Mission accomplished, mother makes all three children happy by buying each one an ice cream cone.

The mother, and even the brother, are pretty good at saying no to sister and coping with the consequences. Mother is especially good at keeping calm and fairly well in control of herself and her whirlwind daughter. She also takes some time to do something the kids enjoy. Sister does indeed come across as a very realistic character. We know that dealing with a live wire like that is definitely not easy.

We need some music here to match the flitty and pesky personality of the little sister. Little Sugar-and-Spice could be portrayed musically by a peppy piano version of Rimsky-Korsakov's "Flight of the Bumblebee," such as the arrangement by Rachmaninov on the cassette, *Flight of the Bumblebee: Virtuoso Piano Showpieces*. Little sister buzzes around indeed with all the speed and annoyance of a bumblebee. It certainly is music to match her personality!

You might ask the children to write or tell a story about what *they* are like when their families take them shopping. Are they better behaved than the girl in this story? Did they ever get lost in a mall? What did they do? How did they feel? What happened?

New Age Music

Let me finish this chapter on relationship stories by looking into some pairing of such stories with New Age music. A children's librarian suggested to me that this contemporary music could work well for story hours, so I found a New Age boutique and made my first purchase: a four tape set called *In Harmony with Nature*, adding nature sounds to classical music. Like most of the tapes in the boutique, this was geared to creating states of peace and harmony, relaxation and meditation. With all the stresses of today's world, it's no mystery why such music is popular. While I'm only a beginner, I felt a mention of this soothing music would be in order here.

There is a picture book called *Johnny Castleseed* by Edward Ormondroyd which is also quiet and relaxed. The relationship of the father and son in it is harmonious. They go to the beach together, where the father shows the boy how to make sand castles and towers and canals. The father compares the process to what Johnny Appleseed did with trees. Other people watching them build sand castles would take away the seed—the idea of how to build them—and their families would wind up making sand castles, too. The boy, in effect, becomes Johnny Castleseed.

On volume one of the New Age tape set, *Gentle Surf*, I found a piece that related well to the water scenes: Vivaldi's Concerto Grosso in A, *Andante* movement, set to a background of ocean waves. Quite a change from my earlier Vivaldi pieces! (The four tapes in the collection set classical music to wind, insects, storms and the sea.) Another tape which I found could also be called a bridge from classical to New Age music, for people reluctant to change their habits all at once. It is called *Pachebel—Music for Meditation: Canon in D, with Nature's Ocean Sounds* by Hari Khalsa. This tape is a modern version of the famous Baroque piece, but with the addition of ocean waves. Certainly this too could be used with a serene scene at a beach such as that in Johnny Castleseed.

✳ ✳ ✳

Ron Hirschi has two very fine picture books on birds that really point out the relationships between wildlife and mankind and the environment. Because they try to build an appreciation of bird life and therefore improve our relationship with these winged wonders, I felt they deserved inclusion here. The books, *What Is a Bird?* and *Where Do Birds Live?* have exquisite photographs by Galen Burrell.

I found a tape advertising itself as "the ultimate in relaxation," called *Mountain Retreat*. Side one contains a field or forest full of twittering birds. This cheerful, chirping background goes well with the bird books, and was certainly different from anything I've tried in the past.

A Sample Arts-Related Story Hour Program
Theme: Relationships
Ages preschool and early elementary

1. *Activity*
   Puppets and finger counting game, "Five Bears in the Bed"

>Five bears in the bed
>And the little one said,
>"I'm crowded, roll over."
>
>So they all rolled over
>And one fell out
>Four bears in the bed
>And the little one said,
>"I'm crowded, roll over."
>
>So they all rolled over
>And one fell out
>Three bears in the bed
>And the little one said,
>"I'm crowded, roll over."
>
>So they all rolled over
>And one fell out
>Two bears in the bed
>And the little one said,
>"I'm crowded, roll over."
>
>So they all rolled over
>And one fell out
>One bear in the bed
>And the little one said,
>"I'm lonely!"

2. *Musical story*
   Story: *The Wednesday Surprise* (Eve Bunting)
   Music: "Liebestraum no. 3" (Liszt)
   Musical mood: Loving, tender

Art: *The Forest of Fountainbleau* (Corot)
The Reading Hour (Rockwell)
Writing project or conversation: Tell about how you learned to read, and who helped you.

3. *Musical story*
Story: *A Chair for My Mother* (Vera Williams)
Music: "Unfinished Symphony" (Symphony no. 8, final movement) (Schubert)
Musical mood: Mixed sweetness and sadness
Art: *Homecoming G.I.* (Rockwell)
Writing project or conversation: Tell about get-togethers in your own neighborhood

4. *Coloring*
Each child can be given a photocopied picture of the five bears in the bed to color and take home as a souvenir.

References

Books:

Berenstain, Jan and Stan. *The Berenstain Bears and the Bad Dream*. Random House, 1988.
Bunting, Eve. *The Wednesday Surprise*. Clarion, 1989.
Finch, Christopher. *Norman Rockwell's America*. Reader's Digest/Harry N. Abrams, 1975.
Hirschi, Ron. *What Is a Bird?* Photographs by Galen Burrell. Walker and Company, 1987.
———. *Where Do Birds Live?* Photographs by Galen Burrell. Walker and Company, 1987.
Mayer, Mercer. *Just Shopping with Mom*. Western Publishing, 1989.
Ormondroyd, Edward. *Johnny Castleseed*. Houghton Mifflin, 1985.
Patterson, Nancy-Lou. *Canadian Native Art*. Collier-Macmillan Canada, 1973.
Say, Allen. *The Lost Lake*. Houghton Mifflin, 1989.

Speare, Jean. *A Candle for Christmas*. Margaret K. McElderry Books, n.d.

Viorst, Judith. *The Good-Bye Book*. Atheneum, 1988.

Williams, Vera B. *A Chair for My Mother*. Greenwillow, 1982.

Yolen, Jane. *Owl Moon*. Philomel Books, 1987.

Cassettes:

Beethoven, Ludwig van. "Für Elise." *Liebestraum: Piano Favourites*. London. Treasury. 417 884–4.

Falla, Manuel de. "Ritual Fire Dance." *The World's Favorite Piano Music*. Philippe Entremont, pianist. Columbia YT 35927.

In Harmony with Nature: An Environmental Experience. Volume one, *Gentle Surf*. (Vivaldi. Concerto Grosso in A). Madacy. C4-5628-1.

Khalsa, Hari. *Pachelbel. Music for Meditation. Canon in D with Nature's Ocean Sounds*. Invincible Music. INV082.

Liszt, Franz. "Liebestraum no. 3" ("Dream of Love"). *Ibid*. Mendelssohn, Felix. *Liebestraum: Clair de Lune, Song Without Words, et al*. Deutsche Grammophon, Musikfest. 413411–4.

Mountain Retreat. Madacy. MR-4 2801.

Mozart, Wolfgang Amadeus. *Concerto for Clarinet*. MCA Classics. MCAC-25965.

Rimsky-Korsakov, Nicolai. "The Flight of the Bumblebee." *The Flight of the Bumblebee: Virtuoso Piano Pieces*. London. 411 836-4.

Schubert, Franz. "Impromptu no. 4." *Song Without Words—Fifteen Best Loved Piano Melodies*. London/Viva. 414 012-4.

Record Albums:

"Alphorn with Cattle Bells." *Swiss Mountain Music*. Capitol. DT 10161.

Beethoven, Ludwig van. "Piano Sonata no. 14" ("Moonlight Sonata"), third movement, *Presto Agitato. Beethoven—Three Favorite Sonatas*. Rudolph Serkin, pianist. Columbia. MS 6481.

Schubert, Franz. Symphony no. 8. ("Unfinished"). *Schubert: Unfinished Symphony and Symphony no. 5*. Seraphim. Great Classical Masterworks. SLP 8034.

12
Waltzes and Wanderings

Here's an intriguing thought—combining stories that take us places with the joyous waltz music of Johann Strauss, Emil Waldteufel, and the other dance music masters.

Let's start with a Peter Spier book that takes the reader as far as his or her imagination can go—*Dreams*. This wordless picture book involves a boy and a girl out in the field watching the shapes of clouds go by and pretending they are horses, chickens, kangaroos, lions, sheep, dragons, knights, boats, swans, trains, and planes. The only words, at the end of the book, urge the reader to look at the sky also and to dream dreams like the children in the book.

When you hear a Strauss waltz, you can imagine dancing couples swirling joyously from one end of the dance floor to the other. In *Dreams* we have a very young couple dancing in their imaginations all over the world and the sky itself and even through time. Dinosaurs cavort with elephants, mythical unicorns romp with seals, flying dragons share the sky with real-life jets, trains fly with propeller planes and real birds. Certainly the swirling, happy music of a Strauss waltz matches this mood very well. Of all the Strauss waltzes, I picked "Roses from the South" because of its lilting, leisurely, and infectiously happy melodies. The mood of the music could indeed be described as "good music for watching the clouds waltz by."

There is a counterpart to *Dreams* in the world of art. Marc Chagall's famous dreamlike painting, *Le Promenade* (1917), depicts a standing Chagall holding wife Bella's hand while she is flying like a flag in the wind. This painting gives us the opportunity to show the story audience that art does not have to be realistic, but instead can be anything the artist wants or can "think up," and that it can really make us feel certain ways, just as music can. This, like many large Chagall reproductions, can be found in the Harry N. Abrams series of art books (*Chagall*, 1973).

For an art project, have the children drawing a happy dream, à la Chagall, with no particular restrictions regarding realism. Give them plenty of colorful crayons or paints, and put the waltz back on to help inspire them.

✳ ✳ ✳

By contrast, Lillian Moore's *Little Raccoon's Night-time Adventure* takes place in the dark woods, as opposed to the wide open, sunlit field of *Dreams*.

Our friend Johann Strauss painted a musical portrait of the woods, with all its shifting moods, in his "Tales from the Vienna Woods." This is not the uniformly cheerful and light "Roses from the South," but rather a piece wherein the mood is changeable, as are Little Raccoon's moods in the story. The baby raccoon is told by his mother to go into the woods, cross the log over the pool, and dig for crayfish on the other side. Well, first of all, it is dark out, so the night and the trees already create an atmosphere of danger and a mood of fear in the story.

Then Little Raccoon sees "the thing in the pool" and his fear turns to panic. (The "thing," of course, is his reflection. If the storyteller holds up a mirror and looks into it, this clarifies the idea for children). His friends the porcupine and the skunk tell him to attack "the thing" with a rock and a stick, but "the thing" is also armed with the same weapons! Little Raccoon runs home to his mother who tells him to smile at "the thing." When he does so, he is delighted to see that "the thing" smiles back. He laughs, and so does the thing in the pool. Knowing now that it is safe to cross, Little Raccoon goes on his way, digs up crayfish, and happily brings them home for the family to devour.

The music of "Tales from the Vienna Woods" shifts moods too, from pensive and spooky to exuberant and sprightly. Nevertheless, the overall tone of both story and music is pleasant—

even suggesting a bird call at one point—and full of action. The two woodsy creations go very well together.

✳ ✳ ✳

Let's take another dance around the sky, like Peter Spier did in *Dreams*. This time, however, it's night and the stars are out and the two skywatchers are a father and daughter. In Anna Grossnickle Hines's picture book, *Sky All Around*, a Daddy takes his little girl to the fields to watch the stars come out. At first, things are fairly scientific: Jupiter is identified, for instance. It doesn't take long, though, for the stars to stir their imaginations. They spot a constellation which looks like a princess's crown and the girl becomes a Star Princess. Soon she is pouring imaginary tea from an imagined kettle, like another constellation formation.

Now the stars become fanciful objects like the clouds in *Dreams*. Butterflies, kites, a sleeping horse, etc. The man finally piggybacks his sleepy Star Princess home.

This slow-paced and sentimental gem of a story needs a slow-paced and sentimental musical background. Our friend Strauss has a waltz for every occasion—this time, the beautiful "Vienna Blood," which conjures up feelings of love for homeland. The father in the book also feels lucky to have his own home and his own daughter. The music and the story may well indeed have been made for each other—or at least made to express very similar feelings. For whatever reason, they go very well together.

✳ ✳ ✳

Now let's try Strauss in a more robust mood, in the "Emperor's Waltz," and match the more vigorous music with a real emperor. We will travel to the Kingdom of Didd and match these kingly tones with the vain hero—His Majesty the King—in Dr. Seuss's picture book, *Bartholomew and the Oobleck*.

In this early Seuss classic, the mighty monarch gets mad at the sky for dropping the same old stuff down all the time -rain, snow, fog, sunshine. He summons his royal magicians to see if they can vary the meteorological menu somewhat. They work their terrible magic up on a mountain, with fire and mouse hair, onions and chairs, whiskers and twigs, etc.

Finally something green starts coming out of the sky. It's called oobleck and it's very sticky. The scene is reminiscent of "The Sorcerer's Apprentice" in Walt Disney's animated *Fantasia*, which came out in 1940, nine years before the Seuss book. In that movie, Mickey Mouse causes a flood by attempting to work some stolen magic on the universe. Paul Dukas's music of the same name dramatizes the episode. In the book we have a sticky version of a rainstorm. The Dukas music weaves its drama and mystery just as well for this upheaval of the universe.

At first His Majesty thinks it's great. He summons his royal bell ringers to ring his bells and declare an official holiday. The green stuff is all over the bell, however, and no sounds can be made. The royal trumpeter is similarly silenced. The captain of the guards tries to eat some oobleck and his mouth is glued shut. People begin to realize that the kingdom is in trouble.

Giant green football-like objects pour down on the kingdom and frighten the lords and ladies in their nightgowns. The royal cook gets stuck to his pots and pans. The royal laundress gets stuck to her royal clothesline. The royal fiddlers get more attached to their fiddles than ever. And to top it all off, the king becomes glued to his throne.

Unable to get to the magicians, page boy Bartholomew Cubbins asks the king to say that he is sorry and that the oobleck is all his fault. These words have a magic of their own, and the dreadful oobleck storm begins to abate and finally disappear.

A tie-in with art here might be our best chance to introduce Paul Klee. Dr. Seuss, with his fantastic creatures and inventions, would probably have loved Klee, whose paintings of *The Twittering Machine* and *The Puppet Theatre* would have looked at home on the walls of Dr. Seuss's house. The latter features colorful child-like depictions of puppet humans and animals, a little girl, a stage, curtains and props in various states of right-side-up or wrong-side-up. They are purely whimsical, but capture the feeling of a puppet show. *The Twittering Machine* features sort-of-birds on sort-of-wires in a sort-of-box—words can't quite describe this one. It is purely fanciful and humorous. Both can be found in Douglas Hall's book, *Klee*, which offers forty-eight large color plates, if you want to show a bunch of these charmers.

Perhaps children could draw their *own* version of a puppet show, as Klee did.

✳ ✳ ✳

Now let's look at one of everybody's favorite "travel" books — Virginia Lee Burton's *The Little House*. In this classic story, the people don't travel—the house does!

The little house had been built in the beautiful countryside, a long time ago, and the man who built it vowed that it would never be sold for gold or silver. Rather it would be passed down from generation to generation. The little house could enjoy the beauty of the changing seasons, the sunshine and the snow, the flowers and the birds and the apple trees.

After a time, however, the lights of the city seem closer and brighter. A road is built in front of the little house. Cars and trucks begin to appear. Then come the gas stations. Houses and large apartment buildings spring up all around the little house, dwarfing it into insignificance. No one wants to live in the tiny dwelling any longer.

Trolleys run past it and subways run underneath it. Its windows are broken and its shutters hang crookedly. It is still a fine house, but it is neglected and shabby until one day, when the great, great granddaughter of the man who had built the little house sees it. She and her husband acquire it and move it to the country, far away from the hubbub of the city. Once more the little house could watch the winter, and feel the fall, see the birds of spring, and bask in the summer sun. The new owners paint it pink and fix up those broken shutters. The moon and stars twinkle above, and everything is once again quiet and peaceful.

One way to set this story to music is to bring in Tchaikovsky's "Waltz of the Flowers," from the *Nutcracker Suite*, at the beginning and the end. The bucolic images of the story match the musical portrait of swaying flowers perfectly. For the middle of the story, however, that music doesn't at all match the frenzy

131

of the encroaching city and roads, trucks, cars, subways, houses and tall apartments. For this we could bring in some of the traffic and city sounds from the parts of George Gershwin's "An American in Paris." Sandwiched in between the "Waltz of the Flowers," this makes a perfect contrast.

This is a story that lends itself to enhancement with toys and puppets on a stage. One little toy house can become surrounded with artificial flowers and birds, followed by plastic sections of dollhouses going up, toy trucks, cars, etc. One doll could represent the young woman at the end who buys the little house.

In looking for a depiction of a house in art, I found one that I thought made a nice pairing with *The Little House*. This is an obviously affectionate painting by Andrew Wyeth called *Her Room*, which shows a room by the water with a table and a shell, and light from the sun streaming in. It's very striking, and appears in *The Art of Andrew Wyeth* edited by Wanda Corn.

An art project to follow this story would be to have the children draw their own house, apartment, or own room.

＊ ＊ ＊

Now let's travel again—this time around the world with one of the great artistic talents in the field of children's picture books, Chris Van Allsburg, as he takes us into the world of *Ben's Dream*.

Two children, Ben and Margaret, pedal their bikes quickly back home when they see rain clouds forming. They both decide to study for their geography test. As Ben studies, he becomes drowsy and starts to dream. The rainstorm makes him dream that his house is floating away in an ocean of water, with him inside. Floating along in the water, the boy sees the Statue of Liberty, Big Ben, the Tower of Pisa, a Greek temple, an Egyptian sphinx, the turrets of Red Square in Moscow, the Taj Mahal, the Great Wall of China, and finally Mount Rushmore—from which President George Washington tells Ben to wake up.

Margaret comes over to play, and they discover that they had the same dream. Ben already knows because he saw Margaret in *his* dream when the sphinx came by.

I wanted an exuberant waltz with a foreign sound for this

story of a madcap "houseboat" geography trip. I settled on Emile Waldteufel's "Espana." Most people know this composer's far more famous "Skaters' Waltz," but they don't associate it with his name. If you do know the "Skaters' Waltz," you know that Waldteufel's music is melodic and vibrant. "Espana" is an exhilerating romp and it certainly seems to add a flavorful foreign touch which matches up quite well with the fantastic voyages of Ben and Margaret.

✳ ✳ ✳

Claire Schumacher's *Alto and Tango* tells of the deep friendship which develops between a singing bird named Alto and a dancing fish named Tango. Leroy Anderson has a charming waltz to go with such a story: the "Belle of the Ball." This can be found in most collections of Leroy Anderson's music as well as in some collections of waltzes, such as *A Waltz Spectacular*.

Alto meets Tango one summer by the sea. The bird sings and the fish dances gracefully in the water. The "Belle of the Ball" sets the tone nicely for this scene as well as the overall story. The singing and dancing continue all through the warm summer and their friendship grows. As the weather turns colder, the two affectionate friends know they must leave each other—Alto for a faraway island with sweet-smelling flowers, and Tango for a warm sea where seaweeds grow.

On their respective travels, they both cry. No one notices that Tango is crying, because he is in the water. The two travel on, past sharks, large birds, fearsome storms, lightning and wind. We have a clue that they are on the same course when we see a ship's captain feeding the bird at the front of the vessel while the cook throws scraps to the fish over the rear of the craft!

Alto laments that the trip would certainly be less of a struggle if Tango were near. The fish has similar thoughts. When the bird falls asleep on his new island, and the fish does likewise nearby in his new part of the sea, they both dream of the other.

In the morning, Alto even sings a song for Tango—wherever his friend may be. Tango recognizes the tune and the two are joyously reunited. They sing and dance again, happy to be to-

133

gether, and the strains of Anderson's "Belle of the Ball" carry them off in a happy finale.

In this chapter we've used some pretty modernistic art from Marc Chagall and Paul Klee. Now, after this story of a bird and fish, let's balance the modern pieces with some from centuries earlier. In fact, Robert Maillard's *History of Art* shows us that ancient Egyptian artists were depicting fish in the Eighteenth Dynasty, in works like *Wild Ducks and Fishes*. Maillard also shows us an extremely sensitive painting by Giotto called *Saint Francis Preaching to the Birds*, a fresco from the fourteenth century.

This gives us a chance to introduce the idea of a wall painting or fresco, a large painting on plaster. Some schools in my local area have come up with a great idea, having children do paintings on the school walls. Some of the more advanced young artists do the overall planning and outlines, on themes such as animals or famous Americans, and the younger ones get parts to paint in, under supervision. The idea of a fresco can also be carried out on large pieces of brown wrapping paper hung or taped up along a wall. It's interesting to point out that Giotto was doing the same type of painting too—700 years ago!

Of course, the older the children, the less chance you have of ruining the room. Plenty of papers, canvas cloths, plastic drop-cloths, etc., would be needed for this. Adults might want to pre-draw the outlines also, before turning the kids loose. Whether you have a carpet or washable tile floor may dictate the wisdom of such a project.

A Sample Arts-Related Story Hour Program
Theme: Fantastic Worlds
Ages 3–7

1. *Musical story*
   Story: *Dreams* (Peter Spier)
   Music: "Roses from the South" (Strauss)
   Musical mood: Dreamy music for cloud watching
   Art: *Le Promenade* (Chagall)
   Art project: Draw a happy dream, à la Chagall
2. *Musical story*
   Story: *Bartholomew and the Oobleck* (Dr. Seuss)
   Music: *The Sorcerer's Apprentice* (Dukas)
   Musical mood: Vigorous, like the emperor in the story
   Art: *The Puppet Stage* (Paul Klee)
   Discussion: Fantasy art, like Klee and Chagall, respectively.
   Art project: Have the children draw their vision of a puppet
   show, as Klee did.

References

Books:

Burton, Virginia Lee. *The Little House*. Houghton Mifflin, 1942.
Corn, Wanda. *The Art of Andrew Wyeth*. N.Y. Graphic Society,
   1973.
Haftmann, Werner. *Chagall*. Harry N. Abrams, 1973.
Hall, Douglas. *Klee*. Phaidon, 1977.
Hines, Anna Grossnickle. *Sky All Around*. Clarion, 1989.
Maillard, Robert. *The History of Painting*. Tudor, 1961.
Moore, Lillian. *Little Raccoon's Nighttime Adventure*. A Golden
   Book. Western Publishing Co., 1986.
Schumacher, Claire. *Alto and Tango*. William Morrow, 1984.
Seuss, Dr. *Bartholomew and the Oobleck*. Random House, 1949.
Spier, Peter. *Dreams*. Doubleday, 1986.
Van Allsburg, Chris. *Ben's Dream*. Houghton Mifflin, 1982.

Cassettes:

Strauss, Johann. "Emperor's Waltz." *Johann Strauss Waltzes.* Columbia/Odyssey. YT 35926.

―――. "Tales from the Vienna Woods." *Ibid.*

―――. "Vienna Blood." *Ibid.*

Waldteufel, Emile. "Espana." *Skaters Waltz: Waldteufel's Beloved Melodies.* Deutsche Grammophon. 413 252–4

―――. "Skater's Waltz." *Ibid.*

Record Albums:

Anderson, Leroy. "Belle of the Ball." *Fiddle-Faddle, Blue Tango, Sleigh Ride—10 Other Leroy Anderson Favorites.* Arthur Fiedler and the Boston Pops. RCA Victor. LM/LSC–2638.

Gershwin, George. *An American in Paris.* Leonard Bernstein and the New York Philharmonic. Columbia. FM 42516.4

Compact Discs:

Dukas, Paul. *The Sorcerer's Apprentice.* Chandos. 6503.

Strauss, Johann. "Emperor's Waltz." *The Beautiful Blue Danube.* Deutsche Grammophon. 413–681–2.

―――. "Roses from the South." *Ibid.*

Tchaikovsky, Peter I. "Waltz of the Flowers" from the *Nutcracker Suite. Tchaikovsky's Nutcracker Suite et al.* Leonard Bernstein and the New York Philharmonic. MYK 37238.

13
A Special Story:
Anne Frank's Teddy Bear

If you told anyone you were planning a story hour based on a story by Anne Frank, they would certainly raise their eyebrows. They would immediately picture something based on the famous *Diary of a Young Girl* and wonder how you could possibly present those events to a preschool group.

It seems to be a little known fact, but Anne Frank also wrote some terrific children's stories while hiding for two years in the secret upper room behind the false bookcase in the building in Amsterdam. "Blurry the Explorer" is an absolutely charming story about a teddy bear, completely appropriate for preschoolers, if told in your own words, in a shorter form. You could read it aloud, word for word, with second graders and up, if you choose. It is dated April 23, 1944, in the year before Anne's probable death in the Bergen-Belsen concentration camp. The final entry in Anne's diary is August 1, 1944.

In her diary, Anne expressed many times her desire to write, and to be remembered. The year 1995 will mark the fiftieth anniversary of her premature death. I think the significance of this story and the fiftieth anniversary will not be lost on children's librarians and teachers, who have an opportunity to tell the tale. It seems to me a very fitting tribute to Anne Frank to present this story to young children, fifty years later. Anne wanted to live on after her death, and this would surely have pleased her.

Of course, if you're working with children in the preschool or early elementary age ranges, you wouldn't want to bring up the Holocaust or Anne's death or even the events of the diary. In my situation, I invite parents, grandparents, and older siblings to stay for the programs. I simply hold up the diary and collected works at the beginning and mention that the story for the children that night was written by Anne Frank. Many of the adults present are aware of the significance of that and are very interested.

If teens and adults are not present, there is no justification for mentioning anything. The story stands by itself.

Speaking as a puppeteer, Anne's story lends itself well to puppets and props. A container of baby powder (or chalky erasers) can be used to raise dust as Blurry sweeps the floor; water can be splashed around in the bath scene; the spanking and the kiss can be acted out and enhanced with sound effects.

First of all, let's look at the story, which you can find in *The Works of Anne Frank*. I wonder if anyone has ever thought what a great picture book it would make. The original is long, however, and it is best shortened if aimed at younger audiences.

Blurry, a teddy bear, becomes tired of his mother's fussing at him and dreams of running away and discovering the wide, wide world. He finally decides to actually leave the little girl who owns him and Mama Bear to embark on his adventure. "I was born to see and experience things," he muses. That was the way to grow up! Adults who know the full Anne Frank story can't help but picture Anne herself thinking those thoughts in her captivity as she wrote "Blurry."

Off goes the bear. Stepping out into the sidewalk, Blurry is overwhelmed by the fast-moving trousers, dresses, skirts, and shoes around him. He can't find the world amidst all this. The puppeteer in me can envision this perfectly. Take your largest dolls and parade them back and forth frenetically around a somewhat small bear, who looks around, up and down, in a confused and annoyed way.

Going through an open door, Blurry meets a very valuable but bored house cat named Muriel. Hoping for some company, this angora beauty asks the bear to stay overnight. Blurry agrees, and Muriel soon gives him a slurpy bath with her tongue that seems to go on for hours.

As a storyteller who uses a microphone, I can tell you two of the most sure-fire laugh-getters a storyteller can use: slurps and kissing sounds! The combination of a cat puppet cleaning the bear puppet plus some loud slurping noises right into the microphone never misses delighting a group of youngsters.

The tired bear eventually falls asleep. In the morning he asks for breakfast, but the fickle cat says no, because she doesn't want her mistress to discover Blurry. Off he goes again, only to find himself picked up by a large dog. He can't cry, for he would choke on the tears. He is helpless in the dog's jaws. After what seems like an eternity, the dog gets bored and drops the bear into the street. Blurry is picked up by a little blonde girl who takes him home with her.

Horrors. She promptly drops him into the bathtub (a cardboard cut-out will do) for a second bath in his brief trip, and tucks him into bed.

Enough of this nonsense, Blurry thinks, and soon makes another escape. This time he is lured into a bakery by the delicious smell of food. Two girls who work there take Blurry in, let him eat, and then make him earn it. They hand him a broom (a whisk broom will do), and tell him to sweep, but the flying dust makes Blurry sneeze. Two full chalky erasers clapped together, behind the stage, shoot up a convincing cloud of "dust," for effect.

Again, using a microphone—which I do because we often have close to 100 in the audience—a sneeze or three from the storyteller is another guaranteed laugh-getter.

Poor Blurry is made to sweep long hours, day after day, and it looks like his great discovery of the world is reduced to this life of forced labor. Little does he know that his family has placed an ad in the local newspaper offering a reward for his return. (*Monopoly* money comes in handy here.)

The girls bring Blurry back to his mother and his owner, Mimi. The girl promptly spanks Blurry for running away, which the puppets can act out while the puppeteers supply loud and generous amounts of *Ouches* and *Ows*. Then Mimi kisses Blurry for coming home safely. A smooch into a microphone is a great effect, but you don't have to have an amplifier of any kind to get a laugh with this. Just ham it up, and have the puppets do the same.

Anne Frank has given us everything we could ask for in a children's story—a lovable hero, adventure, crises, a string of amusing characters and situations, and even a happy ending. It is hard not to wonder if she were aware of the parallels in her own situation—the desire to grow up and be free; the hunger, and finally forced labor. The only safety for Blurry, as for Anne, was to stay with the family as long as that was possible.

For musical background, I've used a tape which combines the light-heartedness of Mozart with a backdrop of whispering winds. The tape is from the previously mentioned four-cassette set called *In Harmony with Nature—An Environmental Experience*. The third cassette plays three Mozart quartets against a wind background. The "Quartet in C Major" works well. The typical good-naturedness of Mozart blends easily with the character of Blurry, and the breeze suggests the outdoor experiences and even a touch of danger.

To add an activity to your program, you can talk a little about the history of the teddy bear. From what I've found, President Teddy Roosevelt was on a hunting trip and his aides arranged to have a bear cub available for him to shoot. The president saw the little animal and refused to shoot it. The story circulated, gained popularity and soon teddy bears started to appear in stores.

I thought everyone in the world knew the song about teddy bears—the "Teddy Bears' Picnic." Thinking this would be easy to locate in a music store, I went in and started searching the children's albums for what I thought would be a standard title on at least several albums. Having no luck, I asked the sales experts—who had never heard of it. Finally one looked it up and found that Michael Feinstein had a version of it on his cassette, *Pure Imagination*.

It turns out to be a lively, dramatic, and humorous version, complete with orchestral backing. This was perfect. I told my regulars to bring their own teddy bears or stuffed animals the week I was planning to do all this and we could have a parade of teddy bears through the library.

Over the years the library's bear collection has grown to two large boxes full, so I could easily stage a picnic of stuffed animals and hand puppets marching, eating (plastic fruit), romping, and finally yawning and sleeping. After the picnic, we also used our collection of bears to lend to anyone who had forgotten his or her own bear, or possibly didn't have one, so they could join in the march through the library as well.

By the way, a parade through the library can be a great event—for the kids, for the surprised adult public, for the parents, and the staff. I keep looking for logical events to give me an excuse to create a parade. On Halloween, everyone can wear a costume. On Saint Patrick's Day (or week) everyone can wear green. The Teddy Bear Parade is another good choice.

The long line of children and parents (grandparents, caregivers, neighbors, etc.) can wind through the tables of studying students, through the older people reading magazines and newspapers, through the check-out area, etc. Generally if you encourage the kids to wave and say "hi" to people along the way, everyone stops what they're doing, waves, and says "hi" back. All the serious and unsmiling faces light up at the unexpected visit of parading kids. (I've not yet had anyone tell us to shut up or remind me, "This is a library!")

Settling back into the story room, I put the lights out and top the program off with a teddy bear movie which our state library has available for loan: a very believable teddy-bear-comes-to-life version of Don Freeman's wonderful picture book, *A Pocket for Corduroy*. This film ties in very well with the Anne Frank story, as both concern the adventures of teddy bears on their own, who are both happily reunited with their own little girls.

A Sample Story Hour Program
Theme: Teddy Bears
Ages 4–8

(The story could be used with older children in a different type of program.)

1. *Musical story*:

    Story: "Blurry the Explorer" by Anne Frank.

    Music: "Quartet in C Major" (Mozart)

    Musical mood: Light-hearted and adventurous, with the sound of breezy wind in the background, suggesting Blurry's outdoor travels.

    Puppets: Two bears, four little girls, a cat, a dog, a woman, various pedestrians.

    Props: Plastic food, sponges (for a bath), cardboard bathtub, whisk broom, chalky erasers, newspaper, play money.

    Activity: Teddy bear parade through the library (or school library, etc.)

    Puppets: All available teddy bears, plastic food.

    Music: "Teddy Bears' Picnic"

    Film: *A Pocket for Corduroy* (based on the book by Don Freeman)

References

Book:

Frank, Anne. "Blurry the Explorer," in *The Works of Anne Frank*. Doubleday, 1959.

Cassettes:

Mozart, Wolfgang Amadeus. "Quartet in C Major." *In Harmony with Nature—An Environmental Experience*. Volume 3: *Whispering Winds*. Madacy. C4-5628-3.

A Special Story: Anne Frank's Teddy Bear

"Teddy Bears' Picnic." *Pure Imagination.* Michael Feinstein. Elektra. 9 61046-4.

Film:

A Pocket for Corduroy. Phoenix Films, 1986.

Final Reflections
on Using Arts with Storytelling

As I write this, many of the night school teachers at the North Miami Adult Center, including myself, are taking a sixty-hour M.E.T.A. course to keep up our certifications. That stands for Multi-Cultural Education Training and Advocacy. Basically it is a course in how to best teach language and content to limited English proficiency (L.E.P.) students. South Florida has such a large number of immigrants from Haiti, Cuba, and other Caribbean and Asian countries that the vast majority of students in our schools speak English only as a second language. The M.E.T.A. course involves strategies for teaching both content and language proficiency at the same time.

One of the things the course stresses is the plentiful use of "realia"—objects, pictures, music, puppets, newspapers, graphs, maps, etc. Another thing stressed is called a "total physical response"—movement, participation, involvement. Still another emphasis is on speaking, writing, and interacting in small groups.

I couldn't help noticing the similarities to many of the arts-related additions to the traditional storytelling described in this book: music, puppets and props, art reproductions, drawing, painting, writing, speaking and discussion, dramatics with masks, poetry, etc. After all, both young children and night school students have a way to go in terms of English language skills. Let's take a final look at what these arts elements can add to storytime.

Whether you refer to the activities in this book as storytelling supplements, or you use the vocabulary of education — "realia," "total physical response," etc.—it boils down to this: We're all looking for ways to make our presentations more interesting, more fun, and more effective as learning experiences.

On this point I'm reminded of librarian Frances Smardo's study, *What Research Tells Us About Storyhours and Receptive Language* (Dallas, Texas Public Library and North Texas State University, 1982). Her research showed that children who attended the regular library story sessions had significantly and consistently higher scores on tests of basic education, including the ability to listen with understanding, than did children who did not go to the library story programs. Listening to a teacher and understanding the lesson are pretty basic and important skills.

Music

I have used music to help create moods for certain stories. I have also used it to help create the atmosphere of certain settings. At times I have used it as Prokofiev did in *Peter and the Wolf*—to identify characters. I have used music to create elements of surprise, suspense, and humor.

Most of the children I work with only hear music from pop radio stations, M.T.V., fast food restaurants, and older siblings' rock or rap recordings. Listed here is some of the most beautiful music I have used in our story sessions, and I now pose the question: "How often, if ever, are most of the children at *your* story hours exposed to these musical pieces?"

> Beethoven's "Moonlight Sonata"
> Handel's "Harp Concerto"
> Mozart's "Concerto for Flute and Harp"
> Mozart's "Piano Concerto no. 21" ("the "Elvira
> Madigan" concerto)
> Vivaldi's *The Four Seasons*
> Chopin's "Les Sylphides"
> Debussy's "Clair de Lune"
> Haydn's "Surprise" Symphony (no. 94)

Liszt's "Liebestraum (no. 3)"
Tchaikovsky's *Nutcracker Suite*

Besides the practical use of these pieces, which I will describe in more detail, let's not lose sight of the fact that we are enriching our programs in a thoroughly *enjoyable* way.

Now before anyone protests about the all-classical nature of the list, let me also mention a few of the *other* composers and performers we have used in our story sessions:

Zamfir	Wynton Marsalis
Miriam Makeba	Boots Randolph
Glenn Miller	Joe "Fingers" Carr
Spike Jones	The Dukes of Dixieland
John Philip Sousa	"New Age" performers
Henry Mancini	

Music is unlimited in breadth and scope. Each of us has his or her own taste and personal collection. Each of us can bring our own unique offerings to enrich these storytelling programs, to create moods and atmospheres in our own ways.

Moods

Over the years in my storytime programs I've used "Colonel Bogey's March" to create a marching beat and mood for the street crossing scenes in Robert McCloskey's *Make Way for Ducklings*. I have matched the sweetness and tenderness of Liszt's "Liebestraum (no. 3)" with Don Freeman's *Corduroy*. De Lage's *Weeny Witch* heroines have been paired with the wild images of Wagner's "Ride of the Valkyries." Curious George's mischief has been accompanied by Mozart's bouncy "Eine Kleine Nachtmusik." The romantic second movement of Rachmaninoff's second piano concerto has backed up the romantic adventures of Eve Bunting's *Valentine Bears*. The list is endless, and the point is clear: Music enhances and reinforces the mood of any story.

Atmosphere

Music can also be used to create atmosphere, which emanates from a setting or place, rather than from a situation. Circus calliope music gives a flavor to circus stories such as Bill Peet's *Ella*. Miriam Makeba's African songs reinforce the authenticity of Marsha Brown's Caldecott winner *Shadow*. In this book we even try an airy selection from Boieldieu's "Harp Concerto" to go along with Chris Van Allsburg's *Polar Express*, as the fantasy train winds up and down mountains on its way to Santa.

The atmosphere of New Age music is often serene, peaceful, romantic, mystical, or suggestive of various environments. Someday perhaps someone will write a book on the possibilities of combining New Age music with storytelling. Suspense

I've used the opening movement of Beethoven's "Moonlight Sonata" to add to the building suspense in *The Spooky Eerie Night Noise* by Mona Rabun Reeves. Brahms's "Lullaby" provides an ironic way of building suspense for the lurking monster in *There's a Nightmare in My Closet* by Mercer Mayer.

Identifying Characters

The boy, the wolf, Grandpapa, the duck, the cat, the hunters, and the bird in Prokofiev's *Peter and the Wolf* all have their own melodies and instruments, and we can do this as well. I've matched Leroy Anderson's "Fiddle Faddle" with Br'er Rabbit, Aaron Copland's "Rodeo" with Pecos Bill, Debussy's "Girl with the Flaxen Hair" with the long-haired Rapunzel. It's a very interesting and creative exercise.

The Element of Surprise

Surprise is a valuable element in good storytelling. When the action suddenly moves fast in a story, as when the roller coaster starts downhill in Carlson's *Harriet and the Roller Coaster*, you can intensify it with some action-packed music like "The Flight of the Bumble Bee," "Can Can," or "The William Tell Overture." Going from no background directly into a few loud bars of such action music will surprise everyone!

Humor

Music can also intensify the humor in many stories. I've used some old Spike Jones instrumentals with Allard's books about the Stupids. Liszt's "Hungarian Rhapsody no. 2" has run along with Isenberg's *Albert the Running Bear*. Stephen Foster's "Camptown Races" has made us laugh even more at Karen Anderson's *What's the Matter Sylvie, Can't You Ride?*

Puppets

The most endearing of the "storytelling supplements" discussed in this book is the art of puppetry. The simple fact is, no matter how beautiful, handsome, charming, dramatic, skilled, and witty we think we are, it's doubtful that any of us can generate half the charisma of an old dog puppet. At least, not to kids. These furry creatures have the ability to attract so much attention, it's a waste to leave them in boxes only to appear at "puppet shows."

Why not let them join you in your regular story times?

A big advantage of this is that you can use volunteers -young or old—to work the puppets, without need of scripts, dialog, or much rehearsal.

Let's take a brief look at what puppets can add to a story.

Visual Motion

No matter how good a version of "The Gingerbread Man" you're using, you can't duplicate the act of dashing across a stage, away from a farmer, a cow, etc., without performance. There is the whole new dimension and movement that puppets and stuffed animals can add behind you while you're telling the tale.

Clarity

Since we're often dealing with very young children, we should remember that certain words we use are not completely familiar to all of them. A simple concept, for example, like the two skunks in the yard at the end of *The Spooky Eerie Night Noise*, may be a bit unfamiliar to some. Those children who do not know what a skunk looks like may be sitting too far back to see the illustrations in the book you're holding. However, if you can put two skunk puppets or stuffed animals together on the puppet stage, you have instant visual clarity.

It's worth stopping to think about. How many words do we

take for granted which are incomprehensible to small children? How much do we assume when talking to *all* children— forgetting that their cultural and linguistic experiences might range widely?

Fun

When you get right down to it, puppets are just plain fun. If you write for catalogs to the different companies which sell them, you can see the hundreds of possibilities for enjoyment in each booklet. Of course, you may be one of those talented people who can make your own, or you can appeal to parents and P.T.A.s for donations of stuffed animals. You can build up a huge menagerie before you know it. At my library, they built an entire room as part of the library addition to house the hundreds of puppets, props, and stuffed animals we've accumulated.

Participation

At our weekly story times there are always children who want to come behind the stage and be in the program. We generally can work them in, and we always introduce our "mighty puppeteers" after the story. This is a two-way street because it gives us more help, and gives them their first toehold over the footlights. It's like "Broadway" to some of these kids!

Puppet Masks

Since the five Chinese brothers (like so many other characters), are very difficult to locate as puppets, masks can be drawn, colored, and cut out from poster board. Be friendly with your local dry cleaner—hangers make great handles!

With kids who want to be in the show in front of the stage instead of behind the scenes, these "live puppets" give a chance for a little creative dramatics. Again, the need for a script and much rehearsal is eliminated, but there's always room for some ad-libs.

Art Works

When our library initiated its framed art reproduction collection, I became interested in taking some of these prints in with me to the story hours. I've also taken books with reproductions in them, if I didn't have access to the larger objects. In doing so, I've used story-related art from prehistoric caves, ancient Egypt, Norman Rockwell's *Saturday Evening Post* covers, Winslow Homer's seascapes, Marc Chagall's dreams, and Albrecht Dürer's naturalistic studies. I've used artists' renderings of pets and their owners from centuries apart.

In this book I've used these as stepping stones to saying a few basic things about Van Gogh's expressionism, Monet's impressionism, Seurat's pointillism, Picasso's abstract art, Giotto's fresco paintings, and all kinds of other artistic concepts. We need not be art teachers to read up on some basic concepts to introduce.

Art Participation

It's one thing to look at a certain type of drawing or painting, and another thing to try it. Locally we have school children involved in painting pictures on school walls, under supervision—a bit like Giotto himself, or muralists like Diego Rivera did. We can show Degas pastel works of ballet dancers, and let children try using pastels. We can ask them to try a topsy turvy dream-world drawing à la Chagall. We could have them try to do a carefully realistic picture of an observed person or plant or animal, like Dürer did with his famous rabbit or even more famous *Praying Hands*. All of these things can be tied into a story. This has been a main thrust throughout this book.

Writing and Speaking

As a part-time English teacher, I know the value of any project that gets students actually *using* written or spoken language, besides just *listening* to it. Throughout this book, therefore, I've tried to add exercises based on the stories or the art works to be used for essays, anecdotes, topics of conversation, or subjects for poetry.

✳ ✳ ✳

150

Final Reflections on Using Arts with Storytelling

I've written two books previous to this—nice, simple, well-organized things. One was on music, one on puppets. Focused and specific. This time I've tried to bring in all kinds of other arts elements as well, in a very loosely organized format. This book isn't as tidy as the other two, but it's been more fun to write. Like life itself, and like the everyday experiences of children, it jumps from one thing to another in no special sequence and with varying degrees of emphasis. Each chapter therefore holds the possibility of surprise, both for the lead storyteller and for the audience. This emphasis on the "creative process" of storytelling is as old as that art itself. So relax, enjoy it, and let it take you and your young listeners wherever you want to go.

Quick Reference Section

As you have seen, sometimes a story is paired with music, or art, or puppets—not necessarily all three. It depends on what the storyteller thinks will help bring the story to life. This quick reference section gives a chapter-by-chapter look at combinations of stories and music; also stories and music plus art works used together.

1. Harp Music and Storytelling

Book: *Harry the Dirty Dog* (Zion)
Music: "Concerto in B-flat for Harp, Strings and Two Flutes," first movement (Handel)

Book: *The Polar Express* (Van Allsburg)
Music: "Concerto in C for Harp and Orchestra," third movement (Boieldieu)

Book: *Tico and the Golden Wings* (Lionni)
Music: "Concerto no. 4 for Harp and Orchestra," second movement (Petrini)

Book: *The Wreck of the Zephyr* (Van Allsburg)
Music: "Flute and Harp Concerto," third movement (Mozart)
Art: *The Boat Builders* (Homer)

2. Puppetry and Hans Christian Andersen

Story: "The Emperor's New Clothes"
Music: "Pomp and Circumstances March no. 1" (Elgar)

Story: "The Real Princess"
Music: "The Wedding March" ("Here Comes the Bride") from *Lohengrin* (Wagner)

Story: "The Swineherd"
Music: "The Blue Danube" (Strauss)

3. Viva, Vivaldi!

Book: *The Big Snow* (Hader)
Music: *The Four Seasons*: "Winter," third movement (Vivaldi)

Book: *The Chick and the Duckling* (Ginsburg)
Music: "Trio in G Minor for Lute, Strings and Continuo," first movement (Vivaldi)

Book: *Henry and Mudge Get the Cold Shivers* (Rylant)
Music: "Concerto in C Major for Mandolin and Strings," second movement (Vivaldi)

Book: *Lemonade Serenade* (Madden)
Music: "Concerto in C Major for Violin, Two String Choirs and Two Harpsichords," first movement (Vivaldi)

Book: *The Little Airplane* (Gay)
Music: "Piccolo Concerto in C Major," first movement (Vivaldi)

Book: *The Midnight Snowman* (Bauer)
Music: *The Four Seasons*: "Winter," second movement (Vivaldi)

Book: *My Mom Travels a Lot* (Bauer)
Music: *The Four Seasons*: "Spring," third movement (Vivaldi)

Book: *A Rose for Pinkerton* (Kellogg)
Music: "Concerto in G Minor for Bassoon," first movement (Vivaldi)

Book: *So What?* (Cohen)
Music: "Concerto in G Major for Two Mandolins," first movement (Vivaldi)

Book: *The Wish* (Hamburger)
Music: "Piccolo Concerto in C Major," third movement (Vivaldi)

4. Papa Bach and Children's Stories

Book: *At Taylor's Place* (Denslow)
Music: "Brandenburg Concerto no. 6," second movement (Bach)
Art: *The Horseshoe Forging Contest* (Rockwell)

Book: *Bedtime for Frances* (Hoban)
Music: "Concerto for Two Violins," second movement (Bach)
Art: *Doctor and Doll* (Rockwell)

Book: *Earrings* (Viorst)
Music: "Jesu, Joy of Man's Desiring" (Bach)
Art: Egyptian earrings; *A Woman with Chrysanthemums* (Degas); *Boating* (Manet); *The Bodhisattva's Bath in the Niranjana River*; *Amithaba with Acolytes*

Book: *Frog and Toad Are Friends* (Lobel)
Music: "Brandenburg Concerto no. 3," first movement (Bach)
Art: *The Peaceable Kingdom* (Hicks), or *The Sleeping Gypsy* (Rousseau)

Book: *Just a Dream* (Van Allsburg)
Music: "Brandenburg Concerto No. 5," third movement (Bach); "Sheep Shall Safely Graze" (Bach)

Book: *Percy the Duck* (Pizer)
Music: "Brandenburg Concerto no. 3," second movement (Bach)

Book: *The Pet Show* (Keats)
Music: "Jesu, Joy of Man's Desiring" (Bach)

Book: *Reuben Runs Away* (Galbraith)
Music: "Brandenburg Concerto no. 6," first movement (Bach)

Book: *To Sleep* (Sage)
Music: "Brandenburg Concerto no. 4," third movement (Bach)

5. Mischievous Characters

Story: "The Little Red Hen and the Grain of Wheat"
Art: *Harvesting Wheat in the Alpilles Plain* and *In the Field* (Van Gogh)

Book: *Splodger* (Dowling)
Music: "The Toy Symphony" (attributed either to Haydn or Mozart's father, Leopold)
Art: *Snap the Whip* (Homer)

Book: *The Tale of Peter Rabbit* (Potter)
Music: "Minuet" by Boccherini
Art: *Girl with a Watering Can* (Renoir); *Young Hare* (Dürer)

6. **Silly Stories with Popular and Jazz Music (and a Couple of Arias)**

Book: *Bird's New Shoes* (Riddell)
Music: "Bird Brain" (Mancini)

Book: *The Birthday Moon* (Duncan)
Music: "Moon River" (Mancini)

Book: *Harry and the Lady Next Door* (Zion)
Music: Arias by Callas, Albanese, Sutherland, etc.
Art: *The Children of Charles I* (van Dyck); *Portrait of Madame Charpentier and Her Children* (Renoir)

Book: *If I Rode an Elephant* (Young)
Music: "Baby Elephant Walk (Mancini)

Book: *Jack and Fred* (Barton)
Music: "Goofus" (Joe "Fingers" Carr)
Art: *Luncheon of the Boating Party* (Renoir)

Book: *Joyful Noise* (Fleishman)
Music: "I Will Wait for You" (Conniff)

Book: *Mrs. Switch* (Hoff)
Music: "Alley Cat" (Conniff)
Art: *Miss Olson* (Wyeth)

Book: *Mucky Moose* (Allen)
Music: "Bassoon Concerto in B-flat Major" (Mozart)

Book: *The Singing Rhinoceros* (Standon)
Music: "La donna è mobile" (Verdi)

Book: *The Three Little Pigs* (Marshall)
Music: "Charlie Brown" (Boots Randolph)

7. Puppets and the Art of Surprise

Story: "The Flying Horse" (Lewis)
Art: *The Green Horse* (Chagall); *The Blue Horse* (Franz Marc)

Story: "How Mr. Rabbit Succeeded in Raising a Dust"
Music: "The Wedding March" (Wagner)

Story: "One Particular Small, Smart Boy" (Lewis)
Art: *The Colossus* (Goya)

Book: *The Popcorn Dragon* (Thayer)
Music: "Puff, the Magic Dragon" (Peter, Paul and Mary)

8. Puppet Masks—Children as Puppets

Book: *The Banza* (Wolkstein)
Music: *Feuding Banjos* (Weissberg)
Art: *Where Art Is Joy* (Rodman)

Book: *The Five Chinese Brothers* (Bishop)
Art: Chinese landscape paintings

Book: *The Real Tooth Fairy* (Kaye)
Music: "Moonlight Sonata," opening (Beethoven)

9. Dog Stories

Book: *Buster and the Little Kitten* (Madokoro/Lauber)
Music: "Six Flute Quartets" (Haydn)
Art: *The Kitchen* and other paintings (Larsson)

Book: *Buster Catches a Cold* (Madokoro/Lauber)
Music: "Six Flute Quartets" (Haydn)
Art: *The Waves at Matushima* (Sotatsu); *Irises and Bridge* (Korin)
Poetry: *A Few Flies and I: Haiku by Issa* (Merrill and Solbert)

Book: *Buster's First Thunderstorm* (Madokoro/Lauber)
Music: "Six Flute Quartets" (Haydn)
Art: Japanese paintings

Book: *Harriet and Walt* (Carlson)
Music: "Bassoon Concerto in B-flat" (Mozart)

Book: *Harry's Smile* (Caple)
Music: "Rialto Ripples" (Gershwin)
Art: *Mona Lisa* (da Vinci); *A Girl and Her Duenna* (Murillo); *The Laughing Cavalier* and *The Fisher Girl* (Hals); *The Shrimp Girl* (Hogarth)

Book: *Lengthy* (Hoff)
Music: "Turkish March" (Mozart)
Art: *Looking Out to Sea* and *No Swimming* (Rockwell)

Book: *Pssst! Doggie* (Keats)
Music: "The Sea and Sinbad's Ship" from *Schehrezade* (Rimsky-Korsakov); African tribal and dance music; Greek music; "Ciribiribin" (James); "Sabre Dance" (Khachaturian); "Coppelia" (Delibes); "Can-Can" (Offenbach); and the "Washington Post March" (Sousa)

Book: *Two Dog Biscuits* (Cleary)
Music: "Concerto for Two Pianos" (Mozart)

10. **Stories That Tug at the Heart**

Book: *Daydreamers* (Greenfield)
Music: "Beautiful Dreamer" (Foster)
Art: *The Dream* or *Reverie* (Chagall)

Book: *Fireflies* (Brinckloe)
Music: "Perpetual Motion" (Paganini) by Wynton Marsalis

Book: *The First Doll in the World* (Pape)
Music: "Piano Concerto no. 21"—the "Elvira Madigan" concerto (Mozart)
Art: Prehistoric paintings from the Lascaux Cave (France) and Altamira Cave (Spain)

Book: *How Many Days to America?* (Bunting)
Music: *Largo* from Symphony no. 5, "From the New World" (Dvorak)
Art: *The Four Freedoms* (Rockwell)

Book: *Jamaica Tag-Along* (Havill)
Music: "Mary Ann" or any other steel drum selections from *Beautiful Barbados*

Book: *Laura Charlotte* (Galbraith)
Music: "Intermezzo" from the *Carmen Suite* (Bizet)

Book: *Music, Music for Everyone* (Williams)
Music: "Lady of Spain" (Floren)
Art: *Women Making Music* (ancient Egypt), *Shuffleton's Barbershop* (Rockwell), and *The Three Musicians* (Picasso)

Book: *Princess Pearl* (Weiss)
Music: *Feuding Banjos*
Art: *The Painter's Daughters* (Gainsborough)

Book: *Song and Dance Man* (Ackerman)
Music: "Me and My Shadow"

Book: *Wild, Wild Sunflower Child, Anna* (Carlstrom)
Music: "Le Garde Montante" from the *Carmen Suite* (Bizet)
Art: *Sunflowers* (Van Gogh)

11. **Relationships—Families, Friends, Animals**

Book: *The Berenstain Bears and the Bad Dream* (J. and S. Berenstain)
Music: "Moonlight Sonata" (Beethoven)

Book: *A Candle for Christmas* (Speare)
Music: *Adagio* from "Concerto for Clarinet" (Mozart)
Art: Canadian native art

Book: *A Chair for My Mother* (Williams)
Music: "The Unfinished Symphony" (no. 8) (Schubert)
Art: *Homecoming G.I.* (Rockwell)

Book: *The Goodbye Book* (Viorst)
Music: "Ritual Fire Dance" (Falla); "Song Without Words" (Mendelssohn)

Book: *Johnny Castleseed* (Ormondroyd)
Music: New Age music. *Pachebel: Music for Meditation. Canon in D with Nature's Ocean Sounds* (Hari Khalsa).

Book: *Just Shopping with Mom* (Mayer)
Music: "Flight of the Bumblebee" (Rimsky-Korsakov)

Book: *The Lost Lake* (Say)
Music: "Impromptu no. 4" (Schubert)

Book: *Owl Moon* (Yolen)
Music: "Alphorn with Cattle Bells" (Swiss mountain music); "Moonlight Sonata" (Beethoven)

Book: *The Wednesday Surprise* (Bunting)
Music: "Liebestraum no. 3" (Liszt) or "Für Elise" (Beethoven)
Art: *The Forest of Fontainbleau* (Corot); *The Reading Hour* (Rockwell)

Books: *What Is a Bird?* and *Where Do Birds Live?* (Hirschi)
Music: *Mountain Retreat* (bird sounds)

12. **Waltzes and Wanderings**

Book: *Alto and Tango* (Schumacher)
Music: "Belle of the Ball" (Anderson)
Art: *Wild Ducks and Fish* (ancient Egyptian); *St. Francis Preaching to the Birds* (Giotto)

Book: *Bartholomew and the Oobleck* (Dr. Seuss)
Music: The "Emperor's Waltz" (Strauss) and "The Sorcerer's Apprentice" (Dukas)
Art: *The Puppet Theatre* and *The Twittering Machine* (Klee)

Book: *Ben's Dream* (Van Allsburg)
Music: "Espana" (Waldteufel)

Book: *Dreams* (Spier)
Music: "Roses from the South" (Strauss)
Art: *Le Promenade* (Chagall)

Book: *The Little House* (Burton)
Music: "Waltz of the Flowers" from the *Nutcracker Suite* (Tchaikovsky); "An American in Paris" (Gershwin)
Art: *Her Room* (Wyeth)

Book: *Little Raccoon's Night-time Adventure* (Moore)
Music: "Tales from the Vienna Woods" (Strauss)

Book: *Sky All Around* (Hines)
Music: "Vienna Blood" (Strauss)

13. A Special Story: Anne Frank's Teddy Bear

Story: "Blurry the Explorer" from *The Works of Anne Frank*
Music: "Quartet in C Major" (Mozart) from *In Harmony with Nature—An Environmental Experience*; "Teddy Bears' Picnic"
Film: *A Pocket for Corduroy*

Resource Directory

Applause
6101 Variel Ave.
Woodland Mills, CA 93167
Puppets.

Brodart Co.
1609 Memorial Ave.
Williamsport, PA 17705
*Puppet theaters, hand
puppets, talking book puppet,
Barney and Baby Bop,
marionettes.*

Constructive Playthings
1227 E 119th St.
Grandview, MO 64030
*Multi-ethnic dolls, just-born
babies, cuddle-kids.*

Country Critters
217 Neosho
Burlington, KS 66839
*Wildlife and domestic animal
puppets and plush toys;
storage racks.*

R. Dakin Co.
PO Box 7200
San Francisco,CA 94120
Puppets, stuffed animals.

Demco, Inc.
PO Box 7488

Madison, WI 53707
or
PO Box 7767
Fresno, CA 93747
*Glove puppets, oceanic
puppets, Madeleine dolls,
insects dragon, Wild Things
and Max, Mother Goose,
royalty, standing puppet
theater, doorway theater.*

Gaylord
Box 4901
Syracuse, NY 13221
Puppets, stages.

The Highsmith Co.
W 5527 Highway 106
PO Box 800
Fort Atkinson, WI 53538
*Storytelling puppets that
swallow, make-your-own-
puppet kits, pop-up puppets,
marionettes, shadow puppet
screen, stage, clowns.*

Lakeshore Learning Materials
2695 E Dominguez St.
PO Box 6261
Carson, CA 90749
Family puppets (African-

American, Asian, Hispanic, White), career character dolls, knit puppets, big mouth puppets, fingerplay mitt kit.

Nancy Renfro Studios
PO Box 164226
Austin, TX 78716
People puppets, royalty, handicapped puppets, fairytale characters.

The Nature Company
PO Box 188
Florence, KY 41022
Bat puppet with 24" wingspan.

Pyramid School Products
6510 N 54th St.
Tampa, FL 33610

Puppets, plastic toys, hats, cymbals, castanets, maracas xylophones, tambourines, triangles, bells, etc., for sound effects.

Russ Berrie and Co.
111 Bauer Dr.
Oakland, NJ 07436
Puppets.

Solutions
PO Box 6878
Portland, OR 97228
Rubber lifelike hand puppets: dogs, pig, cow, elephant.

WatchMe Blossom Theater
  Works
109 SE Alder
Portland, OR 97214
Lightweight puppet theater.